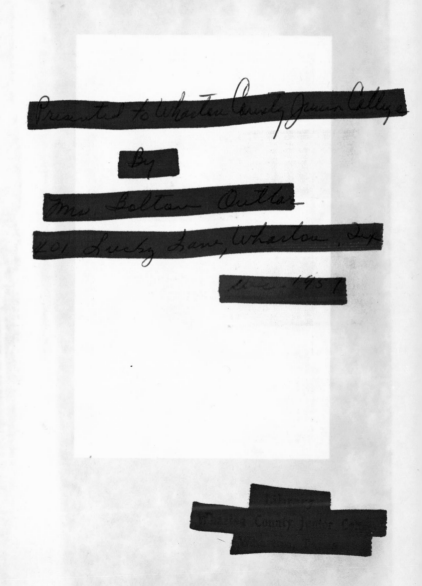

SPEAKING OF MURDER

RANDOM HOUSE, NEW YORK

Speaking of Murder

A MELODRAMA

by AUDREY and WILLIAM ROOS

Photographs by courtesy of Friedman-Abeles

For Steve

SPEAKING OF MURDER *was first presented by Courtney Burr and Burgess Meredith at the Royale Theatre, New York City, on December 19, 1956, with the following cast:*

(*In Order of Appearance*)

RICKY ASHTON	Billy Quinn
CONNIE BARNES ASHTON	Neva Patterson
JANIE ASHTON	Virginia Gerry
CHARLES ASHTON	Lorne Greene
ANNABELLE LOGAN	Brenda de Banzie
MRS. WALWORTH	Estelle Winwood
MILDRED	Brook Byron
MITCHELL	Robert Mandan

Directed by Delbert Mann

Setting and Lighting by Frederick Fox

Costumes by Alice Gibson

SCENES

The Time: The Present

The Place: The entire action of the play takes place in the library of the Ashton home, forty miles north of New York City.

ACT ONE

Scene 1: Late afternoon, early July.

Scene 2: Half an hour later.

ACT TWO

Scene 1: The following Friday, shortly before noon.

Scene 2: Later that afternoon.

ACT THREE

The same afternoon, five o'clock.

ACT ONE

ACT ONE

Scene 1

The Ashton library is a large, high-ceilinged room in a rock castle of a house on the east bank of the Hudson River, north of Tarrytown. It is indeed a library. The walls are lined with book-filled shelves from floor to ceiling. There is a tall library ladder. A staircase on the right of the back wall rises to a small balcony with a door leading to the bedroom floor of the mansion. Beneath the balcony, in the center of the rear wall, there are mahogany louvered double doors— apparently a closet. To the left of it is the entrance from the hall, great mahogany doors in a high, wide arch. The left wall of the room is almost completely taken up by French doors, opening on a terrace. There is a desk with chairs on each side of it, just inside the terrace doors. Behind the desk, in the rear wall there is a small cupboard built into the shelves. In the center of the room there is a long sofa, a coffee table before it, other chairs flanking the table. There is a huge antique grandfather clock. A very feminine effort has been made to "cozy up" the old-fashioned austerity of the room, with chintzes and other gay fabrics.

As the curtain rises, a small dog is resting comfortably on the sofa. RICKY ASHTON, *a boy of nine, is sitting in a wing*

3

chair, reading a book. After a moment, RICKY *suddenly closes the book, rises. He goes to the sofa, sits beside the dog, rubs its ears.*

RICKY

Hello, Joe, what do you know?

> (RICKY *rises and wanders to the desk. Bored, he idly dials the phone without lifting the receiver. The clock strikes four. The phone dial gives* RICKY *an idea. He makes sure that no one is coming, then runs to the louvered doors beneath the balcony. He opens the doors, disclosing the steel door of a walk-in vault. He dials the combination, swings open the heavy door . . . then hears someone in the hall. In his haste to get away, he doesn't get the vault door or the louvered doors completely closed. He runs out to the terrace, disappears.* CONNIE BARNES, *a strikingly beautiful dark-haired young woman in her early thirties, enters from the hall. She puts purse and gloves on the coffee table, sits on the sofa wearily.*)

CONNIE

(Petting the dog)

Hello, Joe, what do you know?

> (JANIE ASHTON, *a robust little girl of seven, steps out onto the balcony. She wears shorts and a T-shirt.*)

JANIE

Hi, Connie!

(She comes down the stairs.)

4

CONNIE

Hiya, Janie. Where are you going in such a rush?

JANIE

I'm going to help Ricky paint his boat. Miss Annabelle said I could. (*She heads for the terrace, then turns back*) Connie, Beverly Hills has been calling you all afternoon.

CONNIE

(*Sighs*)
Thanks, Janie. Is your father in the studio?

JANIE

I think so.

CONNIE

Will you tell him I'm home?

JANIE

Okay!
(*She exits.* CONNIE *pats Joe for a moment, then the phone rings. It rings again before she answers it.*)

CONNIE

(*Into phone*)
Hello . . . Mrs. Ashton? (*She sees* CHARLES ASHTON *coming across the terrace*) Just a moment, I'll see . . .
(CHARLES *enters. He is an attractive man about forty.*)

CHARLES

Connie! How did you get home?

CONNIE

I got a lift. Darling, it's California again . . . tell them
I'm not here . . . anything . . .
(*She hands the phone to him.*)

CHARLES

(*Into phone, enjoying the situation*)
Hello, this is Mr. Ashton. Yes, Operator . . . I know you
do, but she's not here. She's gone on a trip somewhere.
Hudson Bay, I think . . . Won't be back for months.
Sorry . . . Good-bye (*He hangs up, laughs*) California
may never call again.

CONNIE

Darling, I've made that picture eighteen times. There's
always this girl singer . . . or dancer . . . or skater or
swimmer . . . who comes to New York . . . and I'm
always her roommate! Charles, I want to be your roommate!

CHARLES

(*Taking her in his arms*)
Glad to have you, stick around, make yourself comfort-
able . . .
    (*They kiss, then break apart as* ANNABELLE LOGAN
    enters from hall. She is a pretty blonde, nearly forty.
    She is English. She carries a handful of mail.)

ANNABELLE

Connie, why on earth did you walk home? I saw you from my window . . .

CHARLES

You walked home? You said you got a ride.

CONNIE

(*A little laugh*)

That wasn't quite accurate . . . I did walk.

ANNABELLE

Three miles! In those heels!

CHARLES

Why the hell didn't you call me?

ANNABELLE

Yes! You were to call Charles when you finished at the hairdressers.

CONNIE

(*Reluctantly*)

I did. I talked to Ricky. (*To* CHARLES) He said he'd tell you I was ready to come home and I started walking to meet you. Apparently Ricky forgot to tell you.

CHARLES

He forgot to tell me?

7

CONNIE

I'm sure that's all it was!

ANNABELLE

Of course it is! The child's so excited about his boat he can't think of anything else. Connie, the photographer's going to be here at five, sharp. That should give you and Charles plenty of time to get to your cocktail party.

CONNIE

Don't worry about that.

ANNABELLE

The ladies are thrilled that you're going to pose with them! With you in the picture, we'll make the front page. Charles, it was so very clever of you to marry a movie star.

CHARLES

I'd do anything for the Visiting Nurses.

ANNABELLE

Connie, I want you to know how grateful . . .

CONNIE

I'm not doing anything . . . But, you, you've been knocking yourself out for this auction.

(CHARLES *notices that the louvered doors are ajar; he goes to them.*)

ANNABELLE

I can't bear the thought of the Visiting Nurses being without funds. They do such good work.

CHARLES

The vault's open! My God! Who did that?

ANNABELLE

(*Quickly*)

I'm afraid I did ...

CHARLES

(*He closes steel door, spins dial*)

Leaving this thing open is like leaving a loaded gun around.

ANNABELLE

I know, and I'm sorry. I only meant to leave the room for a second. I'm sorry, Charles.

CONNIE

What's all the fuss about?

CHARLES

(*Closing louvered doors*)

I got caught in there once when I was a kid. It scared hell out of me. That damn vault is soundproof, fireproof, dustproof, airproof . . .

9

ANNABELLE

And mothproof. Connie, I thought you might store your furs there.

CHARLES

(*To* ANNABELLE)

Where did you find the combination? I haven't seen it for years.

ANNABELLE

In the desk. It's always been there. I was just checking to see if the vault needed cleaning.

CONNIE

It was built for furs. What's it doing here in the library?

CHARLES

It wasn't built for furs. My father built it for his rare-book collection. The vault cost so much to build, he never could afford any rare books.

ANNABELLE

Connie, I don't mean to rush, but it's time you were changing.

CONNIE

You're right, I'd better start dressing.

ANNABELLE

Oh, Connie, there's some mail for you . . . and for you, Charles.

CONNIE

(*She picks up dog*)

Thanks, I'll see it later. I've got to feed my starving hound before I dress.

(*She exits to hall.*)

CHARLES

(*Starting after her*)

I'll feed your starving hound.

ANNABELLE

(*Halting* CHARLES *by holding out mail for him*) Oh, Charles!

CHARLES

Yes?

(*He takes the mail, goes to the desk with it.*)

ANNABELLE

About Ricky and the phone call . . . You don't really think it was intentional? That he deliberately didn't give you Connie's message?

CHARLES

Three weeks ago I couldn't imagine Ricky doing that to anyone. Now . . . I don't know.

ANNABELLE

I'm certain it was accidental. Oh, there's no denying that he hasn't been very friendly to Connie, but . . .

CHARLES

Friendly! He's been sniping at her ever since she got here! He's made her life miserable.

ANNABELLE

Oh, Charles, Connie understands . . .

CHARLES

How can she? I can't! When the kids were out on the coast, they fell in love with her.

ANNABELLE

Of course they did!

CHARLES

Then what's happened?

ANNABELLE

Children resent change, it frightens them. And you know how secure they've been. We've never had any problems. They were completely happy here with us . . . weren't they, Charles?

CHARLES

I've really handed Connie a job.

ANNABELLE

It's going to be all right. I'm sure of it . . . so sure that I've made my reservations! The *Queen Mary,* a week from Friday. Imagine, after all these years, I'm going home to London once again!

CHARLES

A week from Friday . . . well, Annabelle . . .

ANNABELLE

No, don't make me a farewell speech! Not yet . . . there's plenty of time for that!

CHARLES

I'm not going to . . . but you know how grateful I am. We couldn't have done without you these last three years. Since Elizabeth died.

ANNABELLE

Elizabeth was my friend. To look after her children—your children—I wanted to do that. It's been the most exciting experience of my life. I only wish I could have done a better job preparing them for Connie.

CHARLES

I didn't give you very much time for that.

ANNABELLE

Yes, you did get married rather suddenly, didn't you? Still . . . I might have done more.

CHARLES

Annabelle, this is our problem now . . . Connie's and mine. We shouldn't depend on you any longer.

13

ANNABELLE

I suppose not. You know it hasn't been easy for me to stay on here. But I simply had to, even though I knew my presence here must be an embarrassment to you.

CHARLES

Annabelle . . .

ANNABELLE

No, Charles, it's all right. We're not going into all that again. But I do wish you would realize that our little interlude . . . was no more than that. It meant no more to me than it did to you. You were lonely . . . and I was so available.

CHARLES

(*Taking her hand*)

Annabelle . . .

ANNABELLE

Charles, forgive me. (*She puts her other hand on his*) But I do want you to know that I think Connie is perfect for you, and you know I wish you both the best of everything . . .

(CHARLES *kisses her on the cheek.*)

JANIE

(*On terrace*)

He's in here, Ricky! (*She enters*) Hey, Daddy!

(JANIE *has paint on her face, hands and jersey. She is rubbing at the paint with a rag.*)

CHARLES

Oh, no!

ANNABELLE

Janie, what on earth!

JANIE

Ricky doesn't have any turpentine. He said Daddy might.

CHARLES

Daddy better have some . . . (*He takes Janie gingerly by the corner of her jersey*) or we'll just have to throw Janie away. Come on, baby. I'll take care of you. (*They exit to terrace*) How did such a little girl get so much paint all over her?

> (*They are out of sight.* ANNABELLE *watches them go, puts the letter on the desk, then turns and starts out through the center doors. She stops, and looks thoughtfully at the vault. She opens the steel door, then goes to the terrace doors and steps out.*)

ANNABELLE

Ricky! Oh, Ricky, come here a moment, will you? (*She comes back into room, waits for* RICKY. *He enters*) Ricky!

RICKY

Yes, Miss Annabelle?

ANNABELLE

(*Indicating the open vault*)

Ricky . . .

RICKY

Oh . . .

ANNABELLE

Yes, dear—oh. The reason I never told your father you knew the combination was because you promised me you'd never play with the vault unless I was here in the room with you.

RICKY

I know that . . .

ANNABELLE

But you have been playing with it . . . not just today, either. Often, haven't you?

RICKY

Yes, Miss Annabelle.

ANNABELLE

I understand the fascination it has for you. It is fun, working the combination, isn't it?

RICKY

Yes, Miss Annabelle.

ANNABELLE

Well, close the door now, Ricky, and then you and I will make an agreement. (RICKY *runs to vault, closes the*

steel door and spins the dial) Close it up tightly. (RICKY
closes the louvered doors) That's a good boy. (*He comes
down to her*) Ricky dear, I won't be here to take care of
you much longer.

RICKY

Yes, you will! You're not going.

ANNABELLE

A week from Friday—

RICKY

No!

ANNABELLE

I must, and I want you to make me a brand-new promise,
and this time keep it. So Miss Annabelle doesn't worry about
you when she's far away in London. Promise me you will
never open that vault without permission.

RICKY

Okay.

ANNABELLE

I promise, Miss Annabelle.

RICKY

I promise, Miss Annabelle.

ANNABELLE

All right, you may run along now.

RICKY

Thank you, Miss Annabelle.

> (*He exits to terrace.* ANNABELLE *waits a moment, goes to the vault, checks that no one is watching, then opens the louvered doors. She expertly dials the combination and swings open the steel door. She glances around for a moment, then she exits through the hall doors.*)

ANNABELLE

(*Offstage*)

Joe—Here, Joe. C'mon, Joe. (*She re-enters through hall doors with* CONNIE's *dog in her arms, patting it and talking to it. She goes to vault*) Nice Joe. Nice little doggie. Nice boy.

> (*With a final pat, she puts the dog in the vault, shuts the door, spins the dial and closes the louvered doors. She then starts up the stairs.*)

JANIE

(*On terrace*)

Miss Annabelle, look! Mrs. Walworth is here!

> (JANIE *leads* MRS. WALWORTH *in.* ETHEL *is over fifty, but fighting to look younger than forty. It is a losing battle; her appearance is rather odd . . . so is her manner. She has a shabby elegance about her that is almost comic. She is English. She wears a huge summer hat and carries a gaudy, old-fashioned parasol.* JANIE *is fascinated by her; she keeps inspecting her.*)

MRS. WALWORTH

Annabelle, my dear!

ANNABELLE

(*Surprised, and definitely not pleased*)
Mrs. Walworth . . . well!

MRS. WALWORTH

Yes! Such a day! Lovely! The path through the woods,
you know. (*She looks at* JANIE) The image of her mother
when Elizabeth was her age. God bless you, my dear.

JANIE

Thank you! God bless you, too.
(ANNABELLE *slowly comes back down the stairs.*)

MRS. WALWORTH

(*To* JANIE)

Now, now, children should be seen and not heard. I
so enjoyed taking care of your mother when she was little.
In London, that was. Do you know where London is? (JANIE
nods) And often I took care of your Miss Annabelle when
she came to play with your mummy. Did you know that?
(JANIE *nods*) Cat got your tongue? (*She seats herself comfortably, turns to* ANNABELLE) Well, just a bit of sherry,
perhaps. Or, if that's too much trouble, a gin and tonic.
(*To* JANIE) Run, my dear—ask Mildred to bring me a gin

and tonic, light on the tonic. Run, child! (JANIE *runs into hall and off.* MRS. WALWORTH *turns, watches* JANIE *leave, then turns back to* ANNABELLE) Well, I must say, Annabelle, you've brought her up properly. Where's the new mother?

ANNABELLE

Oh, so you want to see our movie star! That's what brought you here.

MRS. WALWORTH

Not entirely. Though I do admire her, if you like that type. Been married before, didn't you say, off and on?

ANNABELLE

Just once. When she was much too young. There was a divorce.

MRS. WALWORTH

And perhaps there'll be another. Don't despair, he may just tire of her and you'll be Queen Bee here once again. When do they start to build the new house?

ANNABELLE

Soon, quite soon.
(*She sits on the sofa.*)

MRS. WALWORTH

Does she insist? No, she wouldn't have to, if I know Mr. Ashton. Even though it's been in his family—for how many generations?—he wouldn't want her living here . . .

in the shadow of Elizabeth's tragedy. How much better they should start fresh in a nice fresh house all their own.

ANNABELLE

Charles has always meant to build. This old monstrosity of a place is hardly an advertisement for a modern architect.

MRS. WALWORTH

(*Grinning*)

You prefer to think that's it. So galling for you . . . that it isn't to be your new house—yours and his.

ANNABELLE

(*Evenly*)

Just what is it brought you here today?

MRS. WALWORTH

I thought I'd save you a trip this week, my dear. It must be so very tiresome for you . . . trudging over to my dull little cottage week after week.

ANNABELLE

It's a charming cottage.

MRS. WALWORTH

But so expensive. I don't know, I'm not extravagant, but I don't seem able to manage.

ANNABELLE

You're extravagant, my dear.

MRS. WALWORTH

Am I, really? Well, if I am, we just must face up to it. But at the moment . . . a small advance would be so appreciated.

ANNABELLE

I'll bring you your forty dollars on Friday. As usual.

MRS. WALWORTH

You are unco-operative.

ANNABELLE

We have an agreement . . . and you must learn to manage.

MRS. WALWORTH

You've no idea how much lonelier one is when one has no money to speak of . . .

(MILDRED, *a maid in her twenties, enters through hall with a gin and tonic on a tray.*)

MILDRED

(*Extending tray*)
Here you are, Mrs. Walworth.

MRS. WALWORTH

(*Taking the glass*)
Thank you, my dear.

MILDRED

Would you like a cup of tea, Miss Annabelle?

ANNABELLE

Not at the moment, thank you, Mildred. But you might put the kettle on.

MILDRED

(*Going*)

Yes, Miss Annabelle.

MRS. WALWORTH

Yes, do put the kettle on, but don't put the gin away!

ANNABELLE

And close the doors, please, Mildred.
(MILDRED *closes the hall doors as she exits.*)

MRS. WALWORTH

A pretty girl, Mildred, in a dull sort of way. Has she many boys?

ANNABELLE

A few, I think.

MRS. WALWORTH

How far does she let them go?

ANNABELLE

Mrs. Walworth, did you ever have any taste at all? I don't remember.

MRS. WALWORTH

I don't recall, either. But I'm afraid not. It comes from being around children so much. That's one thing I like about the little ones . . . their vulgarity. (*She notices a cigarette case on coffee table. She puts drink down and picks up the case*) What a handsome case, "C. B." Connie Barnes. My, my, Cartier's. Mr. Ashton give it to her?

ANNABELLE

No, she'd had it before that.

MRS. WALWORTH

Must be worth a pretty penny. Three hundred dollars? Even more? Four hundred? Five?

ANNABELLE

I've no idea. Put it down, my dear.

MRS. WALWORTH

Such a handsome thing. Makes one wish one smoked. I suppose one could learn.

(*She opens her purse, drops the cigarette case inside.*)

ANNABELLE

(*Quietly*)

Put it back where you found it, dear.

MRS. WALWORTH

(*Significantly*)

I had another letter from Lucinda Marsh . . . You remember little Lucinda . . .

ANNABELLE

Don't bother going through that again. Really, you can be so very tiresome.

MRS. WALWORTH

I'm just as bored with it as you are, my dear. But unfortunately, it does seem necessary every so often to refresh your memory about Lucinda and her letters.

ANNABELLE

But I can't let you have your way this time. How shall I explain it?

MRS. WALWORTH

Easily, my dear. You're so clever. You were always the clever one. Elizabeth, the pretty one who got all the boys. And Lucinda was the thoughtful one. I only took care of her a year or so after I left Elizabeth. But she still writes to me! After all these years! How very thoughtful. (*She takes blue air mail letter from purse as* ANNABELLE *rises*) Her writing hasn't improved since she was nine . . . (*She reads*) ". . . and give all my love to little Beebee. (AN-NABELLE *moves slowly away from* MRS. WALWORTH, *controlling her impatience*) It must be such a comfort to Mr. Ashton that Beebee is still there. I can imagine how wonderful she is with the children. I should like a snapshot of little Ricky and Jane. Do they resemble their mother? Elizabeth was the prettiest girl . . ."

ANNABELLE

(*Turning to her suddenly*)

Must you? I was never a great admirer of Lucinda's letters!

MRS. WALWORTH

You're right, it is a dull letter, very dull. Except that some people think Beebee was Elizabeth's nickname. That isn't dull. Is it, Beebee?

ANNABELLE

(*She goes to* MRS. WALWORTH, *speaks very quietly, ominously*)

Don't! Don't call me that!

MRS. WALWORTH

(*Quickly moving letter away from* ANNABELLE)

Oh, no, my dear, it wouldn't do you any good to take this letter from me. You know that. I have dozens of them and God willing, I shall get dozens more. Sit down, Annabelle, and don't make it necessary for me to call you Beebee. (ANNABELLE *moves slowly away from her again and sits in wing chair.* MRS. WALWORTH *smiles, goes on, brightly*) How will you explain it? I'm curious. About the cigarette case, I mean. Please don't blame it on the servants. Someone was telling me only recently that in Charles's father's day there were fifteen here in help. . . .

ANNABELLE

(*Almost to herself*)

I'm not at all sure I'm going to let you take that case.

MRS. WALWORTH

Really, my dear, can't we consider that settled?

ANNABELLE

I'm not at all sure. (*Rises, extends hand to* MRS. WAL-WORTH) Give it to me, or I shall call Connie down.

MRS. WALWORTH

How tiresome you can be, Annabelle. You were as a child too . . . so persistent . . . Persistence isn't charming, you know.

> (ANNABELLE *opens the hall doors, steps into the hall, and calls upstairs.*)

ANNABELLE

Connie! Connie, could you come down a moment? (*Comes back to* MRS. WALWORTH, *extends her hand*) Give it to me! She's on the stairs.

CONNIE

(*Offstage*)

Yes, Annabelle.

> (MRS. WALWORTH *hesitates, then quickly hands the case to* ANNABELLE *as* CONNIE *enters from hall.*)

27

ANNABELLE

(*Turning to* CONNIE)

Connie, this is Mrs. Walworth. She was so anxious to meet you.

MRS. WALWORTH

(*Going to* CONNIE)

Yes, my dear. I insisted that Annabelle call you down. Wasn't that bold of me?

CONNIE

I'm glad you did, Mrs. Walworth. I've been looking forward to meeting you.

MRS. WALWORTH

Oh, then you know about me?

(MRS. WALWORTH *sits on the sofa.* CONNIE *sits beside her.* ANNABELLE *goes to the desk, puts the cigarette case on it.*)

CONNIE

You were Annabelle's nurse, weren't you?

MRS. WALWORTH

No, Elizabeth's. Elizabeth and Annabelle were childhood friends, you see. . . . I'm so very happy about you and Mr. Ashton, my dear. It's lovely having him happy again. (*There is a slight pause*) Poor Elizabeth . . . to go so young, so tragically. Just when everyone thought she was getting well again at last. And it was a shock to me . . . to think

that my gay, sweet little Elizabeth could have become that
despondent . . .

Connie . . . Mrs. Walworth . . .

MRS. WALWORTH

(*Rushing on. Including* ANNABELLE, *now*)

Poor Annabelle was staying with Elizabeth when she was
taken ill, you know, and she saw it happen. The green bedroom, you know, with the balcony over the gorge. Those
frightful rocks down below. Annabelle must have had some
premonition about her friend that night. She went to Elizabeth's room to see if she was all right . . .

ANNABELLE

Mrs. Walworth, really, it seems to me . . .

MRS. WALWORTH

It was so heroic of Annabelle. (*She rises*) Yes, it was,
Annabelle. She saw Elizabeth climbing the railing . . . and
she almost reached her in time. Everybody in the house
heard Annabelle screaming to Elizabeth . . . "No, Beebee
. . . don't, Beebee . . . stop, Beebee . . ." And that was a strange
thing you know . . . Annabelle calling Elizabeth Beebee.
. . . She said that in her fright she had reverted to Elizabeth's childhood nickname, Beebee. (*To* ANNABELLE) You
hadn't called her that in years, had you, dear? (MRS. WAL-
WORTH *steps to desk, picks up cigarette case, hides it under
shawl.* ANNABELLE, *defeated, moves away to door*) Mrs.

29

Lawson . . . she used to cook here . . . (MRS. WALWORTH
sits beside CONNIE) she says she can still hear Annabelle
screaming to Elizabeth . . . she'll never forget it. "No, Beebee . . . Beebee, no . . ."

(MRS. WALWORTH *covers her face with her hands.*)

CONNIE

Please, Mrs. Walworth, I know you don't realize, but . . .

MRS. WALWORTH

Oh, I am sorry! (*To* ANNABELLE) Please forgive me.
(*To* CONNIE) It's true, I didn't realize. . . . I do get
carried away. Harry always said I was the one in the family
should have been on the stage. Harry was a baritone.

CONNIE

And your husband?

MRS. WALWORTH

Yes. For quite a while, in fact. We came to America together twenty years ago. I've often wondered what ever
came of Harry. I suppose you never ran into a Harry Walworth, did you? Nice-looking baritone? Could play small
speaking parts?

CONNIE

No, I don't think so.

MRS. WALWORTH

It's just as well. Filthy temper. Harry had such a filthy temper. (CONNIE *rises*) Well, my dear, I do hope you'll visit me some day soon.

CONNIE

I want to very much. Annabelle's told me about that fabulous garden of yours. I'd love to see it.

MRS. WALWORTH

Why don't you come over this Friday . . . when Annabelle comes?

CONNIE

I'm afraid I have a television thing that night.

MRS. WALWORTH

Really? What?

CONNIE

A quiz show . . . I'm on it to plug my last picture . . . and it does need to be plugged.

MRS. WALWORTH

Otherwise I'm sure you wouldn't be caught dead in the television. Such a ghastly invention! And now it's keeping you from calling on me Friday.

CONNIE

I'll come as soon as I can, I promise. Joe and I will walk over some afternoon.

MRS. WALWORTH

Joe? Who may I ask is Joe? Not that he isn't welcome.

CONNIE

Nobody important. Just a little old dog of mine. (*She glances around room*) He's around here some place. (*To* ANNABELLE) Have you seen him, Annabelle?

ANNABELLE

He's with the children, I think.

CONNIE

I'll take a look. (*She starts toward terrace*) I'll see you again soon, Mrs. Walworth.
(*She exits.*)

MRS. WALWORTH

Yes, indeed. (*Looking after* CONNIE) Vital. Good peasant stock, I should imagine. But not half Elizabeth's class though. Well, my dear, it's no effort to be pleasant, is it? (*Puts cigarette case into purse*) We won't quarrel any more. It wasn't really a quarrel though, was it? Just a misunderstanding.

ANNABELLE

(*Quietly*)

I find you very amusing, Mrs. Walworth. That scene with Connie. You should have been an actress . . . But I warn you . . . don't try it again.
(RICKY *enters from hall*.)

32

RICKY

Where's Connie? I thought I heard her in here.

ANNABELLE

She's gone out to look for Joe. Why did you want her?

RICKY

I was supposed to tell Dad that she was ready to come home and . . .

ANNABELLE

Yes, and you forgot, didn't you?

RICKY

Is she mad?

ANNABELLE

Ricky, say hello to Mrs. Walworth.

RICKY

Hello, Mrs. Walworth.

MRS. WALWORTH

That's a good boy.

ANNABELLE

(*To* RICKY)

You can hardly expect Connie to be pleased, dear. Such a long hike on a hot day.

RICKY

(*Stricken*)

Did she have to *walk?*

ANNABELLE

All the way, yes.

RICKY

I better tell her I'm sorry . . .
(*He starts toward terrace.*)

ANNABELLE

Ricky!

RICKY

(*Turns back*)

Yes, Miss Annabelle?

ANNABELLE

The damage has already been done and I'm afraid it
won't make Connie any less annoyed with you. I shouldn't
bother her, if I were you.

RICKY

(*Sullen*)

All right, I won't apologize. That's all I've been doing
ever since she got here anyway . . . apologizing.

ANNABELLE

(*With a great sigh*)

I know it's difficult for you. But you must realize, my
dear, I've tried often enough to explain it to you . . .

34

Connie isn't used to children. She's an actress. Actresses aren't like other mothers. You must learn to be quiet, for instance. You can't go screaming about the house in the morning like wild Indians any more, you and Janie.

RICKY

We've got to have *some* fun. . . .

ANNABELLE

In a different way, Ricky. Now that Connie's here things will naturally have to be a little different.

RICKY

(*Resentfully*)

I won't move. When I'm in the house, I'll whisper. She can sleep all day if she wants to. I'll pretend I'm dead.

ANNABELLE

Now, now . . . you know it would hurt Connie to hear you say that.

RICKY

Well . . . (*He decides to skip it*) Can I go work on my boat now?

ANNABELLE

I'm afraid you're not to work on your boat any more today. That might help you to control your feelings . . . to be a little more understanding about Connie and a great deal less rude.

35

RICKY

But I've got to work on my boat! I'll never get it finished!

ANNABELLE

I'm sorry.

RICKY

(*Turns away*)

I can't do anything any more . . . Not with her here.
(ANNABELLE *reaches out and takes his arm and brings him back to her.*)

ANNABELLE

Be patient . . . it will be much better in a little while, I promise you.

RICKY

No, it won't! When you go back to London next week, it'll be worse! A lot worse!

ANNABELLE

Please, darling . . .

RICKY

(*Pulling away from* ANNABELLE)

I don't care! Everything was fine until she came . . . I don't care.
(*He runs out.*)

ANNABELLE

Ricky! (*But he is gone*) Oh, dear, he is a problem . . .

MRS. WALWORTH

You're leaving for London next week? You'd led me to believe it wouldn't be nearly so soon.

ANNABELLE

Did I?

MRS. WALWORTH

I was under the impression that we had plenty of time to make our arrangements. We do have arrangements to make, you know.

ANNABELLE

(*Rises*)

I'm so sorry you don't have time for another drink before you go.

MRS. WALWORTH

Now don't be unfriendly. What will you do in London? (ANNABELLE *closes hall doors*) Oh, your income is enough to manage my forty a week. I've no fears about that. But in order to live as you've become accustomed to here, you'll need some sort of job to earn a bit extra.

ANNABELLE

I can hardly believe you're seriously worried about my comfort.

MRS. WALWORTH

Interested, not worried. I couldn't really worry about anyone as resourceful as you are, my dear.

ANNABELLE

Thank you so much.

MRS. WALWORTH

You are resourceful, Annabelle! No one would think it to look at you. You don't look at all the type to organize and manage . . . and push people off balconies, do you, dear?

ANNABELLE

If anyone heard you say that, it would end your forty a week, you know.

MRS. WALWORTH

Yes, I do know that. Really, I am careful.
(*She takes a drink.*)

ANNABELLE

I do wish you'd stop drinking so much.

MRS. WALWORTH

It isn't so much. It doesn't seem nearly enough. But I will try.
(*She takes another drink.*)

ANNABELLE

At least try to confine it to the privacy of your charming cottage. Pub-crawling is such a disreputable habit.

38

MRS. WALWORTH

(*Putting drink on coffee table*)

Has Mr. Ashton given you a going-away present yet? A handsome sum, perhaps?

ANNABELLE

No.

MRS. WALWORTH

But he will, of course. And the moment he does, I shall expect you to remember me.

ANNABELLE

Charles's present to me is a first-class passage on the *Queen Mary.*

MRS. WALWORTH

(*Squawking with laughter*)

Absolutely the last thing in the world you wanted! But I've no idea why I'm laughing. (*She rises*) That cuts my throat a bit, you know. Do you think you might borrow . . . oh, say, ten thousand dollars from Mr. Ashton? For me?

ANNABELLE

No, I don't think so.

MRS. WALWORTH

We could call our account settled then. It's been so degrading for you to come trotting to me every Friday with your two little twenty-dollar bills.

39

ANNABELLE

You're being so very thoughtful, Mrs. Walworth. How unlike you.

MRS. WALWORTH

It's not possible for you to send money from England, you know. The only solution is for you to speak to Mr. Ashton. Ten thousand dollars . . . would mean nothing to him.

ANNABELLE

We'll discuss it some other time. At your place.

MRS. WALWORTH

It wouldn't be asking much. It isn't as though you'd been on the payroll, my dear. Really, how could he be so ungrateful? Why, you could even ask a little more. . . . Eleven thousand. Perhaps even eleven-five. I won't let you leave for London without settling up with me.

ANNABELLE

(*Slowly*)

My dear Mrs. Walworth, I'm not going back to London.

MRS. WALWORTH

Not? Oh, but I'm afraid you must. There's no need for you any more, not with the movie actress here.

ANNABELLE

The movie actress won't be here for long.

MRS. WALWORTH

Oh, perhaps I see. You're trying to drive her away. That's why you've turned the boy against her. You mean to break up the marriage.

ANNABELLE

No, I couldn't do that. I don't believe that could be done. It will have to be something else . . . something more than that.

(MRS. WALWORTH *rises, horrified, then recovers as* MILDRED *raps on the door.* MILDRED *enters.*)

MILDRED

It's the photographer from the paper, and two of the ladies.

ANNABELLE

Oh, yes.

(*She goes to the desk and gets a list.*)

MILDRED

They're on the front terrace, Miss Annabelle.

ANNABELLE

I'll be right out.

MILDRED

Yes, ma'am.

(MILDRED *exits.*)

ANNABELLE

(Brightly)

Mrs. Walworth, you must excuse me. The picture for the Visiting Nurses' auction, you know. Now do run along home, dear. Do be charming.

(She exits to hall doors.)

*(*MRS. WALWORTH *sits rigidly, then her head turns slowly toward the terrace as she hears* CONNIE *calling, "Here, Joe . . . here, Joe boy, here, baby . . .")*

Curtain

Scene 2

The Library. Half an hour later.
As the curtain rises, CHARLES *is sitting on the sofa, read-ing.* CONNIE *enters from terrace.*

CHARLES
(*As she enters*)
Get your picture taken?

CONNIE
Got my picture taken. It was fun.
(*She sits beside* CHARLES *on the sofa.*)

CHARLES
Of course it was fun. You were the star.

CONNIE
I'd say Annabelle and I co-starred. She's a big wheel in the Visiting Nurses. Charles, she's leaving next week?

CHARLES
Friday. The *Queen Mary.*

CONNIE
It's definite then? (CHARLES *nods*) I'm glad she's going. Oh, I know how wonderful she's been, all she's done for

the children, but I can't help it. I wish she were leaving sooner. Is that an awful thing to say?

CHARLES

Of course not. I know exactly how you feel . . .

CONNIE

I feel as though I were a guest here . . . and not a very welcome one. I think Ricky and I could get together once Annabelle's gone . . .

CHARLES

It's only another week. . . .

CONNIE

It's going to be a long week!

CHARLES

Maybe I could get the *Queen Mary* to sail a couple of days earlier.

CONNIE

Oh, don't pay any attention to me. Maybe I'm just passing the buck because I haven't made the grade with Ricky. But I will. . . .

CHARLES

All you need is a little time, that's all.

CONNIE

I've always got along with kids. We like each other, kids and I.

CHARLES

Of course you do.

(*He kisses her quickly as voices are heard on terrace.*)

CONNIE

Darling, don't get involved. Run. I'll be along in a minute.

CHARLES

(*Going*)

All right. I'll get the car out. (MRS. WALWORTH *enters through terrace doors and meets* CHARLES) Mrs. Walworth! How are you?

MRS. WALWORTH

Splendid! Congratulations, Mr. Ashton. I'm sure you'll be very happy, you and Connie.

CHARLES

Thank you.

MRS. WALWORTH

What a lovely tie clasp you have there!

CHARLES

Thank you very much.

MRS. WALWORTH

Perfectly lovely. Take care of it.

(CHARLES *exits*. RICKY *enters from hall with a gin and tonic*.)

MRS. WALWORTH

(*Taking drink from him*)
You're a dear boy. What took you so long?
(*She takes a sip*.)

RICKY

I made it myself. Is it all right?

MRS. WALWORTH

Very nice. I hope you do your lessons half as well.

(ANNABELLE *enters from terrace*.)

ANNABELLE

Connie, you inspired our photographer. He was thrilled. Thanks so much for posing with us.

CONNIE

I enjoyed it.

ANNABELLE

I imagine that dress photographs beautifully. You must take it with you on Saturday. (*She sits*) Charles and Connie are invited to Pawling for the week-end.

RICKY

(*Turning to* CONNIE)

You're going away on Saturday.

CONNIE

Yes, Ricky, why?

RICKY

The carnival's this week . . . the Kiwanis carnival. My father always takes us on Saturday.

ANNABELLE

He'll take you another day.

RICKY

But the Death Defying Leap is only on Saturday. I can't miss that!

CONNIE

I didn't know that, Ricky. Maybe we could arrange to . . .

ANNABELLE

Sweetie, this could be terribly important. Mr. Jackson could be one of your father's biggest clients. You do understand, don't you? Mr. Jackson wants to see your father's plans for his new building . . . and he wants to meet Connie.

47

RICKY

On Saturday?

ANNABELLE

Yes, dear. On Saturday.

RICKY

(*Turning away*)

Gee, I always see the Death Defying Leap . . . it's a habit I have . . .

(*He sinks unhappily into a chair.*)

ANNABELLE

Now, now, Ricky. (JANIE *enters on balcony wearing* CONNIE'S *green shawl, white gloves, and carrying her green purse. She glides downstairs*) Well, look at us! Aren't we stunning!

JANIE

Thank you, Miss Annabelle. You should see me in Connie's mink coat. She's going to let me wear it when I get big enough, aren't you?

CONNIE

(*Taking gloves from* JANIE)

It's yours for the Junior Prom, Janie, that's a deal.

ANNABELLE

Mrs. Walworth, Connie's mink . . . it's fabulous . . . (*To* CONNIE) You must be very proud of it.

48

CONNIE

(*Taking shawl*)

Frankly, I am proud of it. It's the story of my life. I earned it all by my little self . . . by getting up early in the morning, not staying out late at night. (*Automobile horn blows*) Oh, Janie, is Joe upstairs?

JANIE

No.

CONNIE

(*Putting on gloves*)

Did you look under my bed?

JANIE

(*Nodding*)

Every place. He isn't up there, I'm sure.

CONNIE

Where could that little mutt be? (*Takes purse from* JANIE) He might have wandered off some place . . .

ANNABELLE

He's around some place. The children will find him.

JANIE

I'll look outside for him. (*She starts running toward terrace*) 'Bye, have a good time.

(*She exits.*)

49

CONNIE

Thank you, Janie.

ANNABELLE

Ricky, you go help Janie look for Joe.

RICKY

Okay!
(*He rises and starts out.*)

ANNABELLE

(*Halting* RICKY)
And what do you say?

RICKY

(*Begrudgingly*)
Good-bye. Have a good time.
(*He exits.*)

ANNABELLE

(*Shaking her head, laughs*)
Yes, Connie, good-bye, have a good time.

CONNIE

Since Ricky insists, I will. Mrs. Walworth, I *am* coming over to see you.

MRS. WALWORTH

(*Rising*)
Soon, I hope.

CONNIE

Very soon. Good-bye, we won't be late.

ANNABELLE

Good-bye, Connie.
(CONNIE *exits. Mrs. Walworth checks that* CONNIE
*has gone, goes to the hall doors, closes them, and
then comes back to Annabelle, who is sitting on the
sofa.*)

MRS. WALWORTH

I absolutely forbid you even to consider it.

ANNABELLE

(*Rising*)

I suppose it was too much to hope you'd go home.

MRS. WALWORTH

I know how much you love him. You'd stop at nothing
to get him back. But you mustn't do it. You mustn't!

ANNABELLE

If there were a less difficult way to get rid of her, I'd
be very happy.

MRS. WALWORTH

I know how you must loathe her, but you won't listen
to me.

ANNABELLE

I don't loathe her at all. I find her charming. But when someone takes what belongs to you . . . you do what is necessary to get it back.

MRS. WALWORTH

I know . . . you've decided he's yours . . . just as you did with little Lucinda's doll. You remember kidnapping Lucinda's doll and hiding it away, don't you? You still don't think that was naughty of you, do you? You still don't think it was wrong about Elizabeth, do you? Naughty, right and wrong . . . such silly words, aren't they?

ANNABELLE

Coming from you, dear, they're hilarious!

MRS. WALWORTH

What do you mean by that?

ANNABELLE

Blackmail, my dear, is such a degrading occupation.

MRS. WALWORTH

One must make a living. It's hardly fair of you to criticize me for being too proud to go on relief.

ANNABELLE

Finish your drink and run along. I do wish you would.

MRS. WALWORTH

You might have a little consideration for me. (*She sits*) Something might go wrong, and with you in prison . . . there goes my forty a week!

ANNABELLE

Nothing shall go wrong. I hope you've made no plans for Friday . . . this Friday.

MRS. WALWORTH

You aren't thinking of . . . you're not expecting to go about it this Friday!

ANNABELLE

Yes, it has to be then. Friday I shall expect you to spend the afternoon in your cottage . . . alone. Are your gladiolas in bloom?

MRS. WALWORTH

My gladiolas?

ANNABELLE

I shall need a rather large bouquet. You must bring them over here about noon on Friday. You'll hide them behind the old carriage house. Be very careful that no one sees you.

MRS. WALWORTH

Incredible! You even hoped I would become an active accomplice!

53

ANNABELLE

You will be running no risk whatsoever. (*Pauses, then rises and goes to terrace doors*) Ricky! Oh, Ricky, dear, would you come in please, for a minute? (*She comes back to the desk, smiles significantly at* MRS. WALWORTH. RICKY *enters*) Ricky, did you find Joe? (*He shakes head*) Is Janie still looking for him?

RICKY

Yes. Do I have to? Can't I work on my boat?

ANNABELLE

(*Opening louvered doors of vault*)
Ricky, dear, would you help me? I want to use the vault for storage. Would you open it for me?

RICKY

(*Running to vault*)
Gee, thanks!
(MRS. WALWORTH *watches closely, wondering what* ANNABELLE *is up to.* RICKY *is working the combination.*)

ANNABELLE

(*To* RICKY)
Having trouble, dear?

54

RICKY

No, I've got it . . . (*Swings open the steel door*) There!

ANNABELLE

Good boy. I suppose it does need a good clean out, doesn't it?

RICKY

I don't know . . . (*Steps into vault to see. A pause*) Miss Annabelle! Come here, quick! !

ANNABELLE

(*Hurrying to vault*)

What is it, dear?

RICKY

(*Crying. Still inside vault*)

It's Joe!
(MRS. WALWORTH *steps closer.*)

ANNABELLE

Oh, Ricky, no . . . (*She swings* RICKY *away from vault*) Don't look, dear. He's dead!
(MRS. WALWORTH *turns front.*)

RICKY

How did it happen? How did Joe get in there?

ANNABELLE

(*Puts her arm around him*)

You poor child. You don't even realize what you've done, do you?

RICKY

What?

ANNABELLE

(*Hugging* RICKY *to her*)

Ricky, Ricky, Ricky . . . you were a naughty boy. You opened the vault . . . you left it open for quite a while. Little Joe crawled in . . . perhaps he went to sleep, I don't know. But when you closed the door . . .

(MRS. WALWORTH *sits slowly on the sofa.*)

RICKY

You told me to!

ANNABELLE

Yes, and when you did, little Joe couldn't breathe. Nobody could hear him barking . . . poor little thing. He suffocated . . . (*She holds him off at arm's length*) because you were a naughty boy and played with the vault. You did it, Ricky.

RICKY

No, no! I didn't see him go in. I . . .

ANNABELLE

Of course you didn't see him go in! You didn't do it intentionally. It was an accident. But you did do it.

RICKY

What will happen? What will they do to me?

ANNABELLE

(*Releasing* RICKY *and moving away from him*)
I don't know. I don't know what they'll do . . . but they'll be very, very angry. It was a naughty thing you did.

RICKY

But I didn't mean to do it.

ANNABELLE

Do you think they'll believe that? You haven't been very nice to Connie, you don't like her. Your father knows that I'm afraid he may think you did it on purpose.

RICKY

(*Going to her*)
Oh, no, it was an accident! You'll tell them that, won't you, Miss Annabelle?

ANNABELLE

(*Takes his hands*)
Will that do any good, dear? But I'll help you, Ricky. I'll think of something. What can I do? What ever can I do? I

57

know. We won't tell them little Joe got caught in the vault, because then they'd know you did it. I have it! I'll put him out on the lawn . . . perhaps they'll think he was hit by a car. Something like that.

RICKY

Yes!

ANNABELLE

All right, dear. Go up to your room now. (*She smoothes his hair*) You're hot and upset. You must rest a little. Go up and lie down for a while. Everything will be all right, I promise.

RICKY

Yes, Miss Annabelle.
(*Sobbing, he runs up the stairs and out. There is a pause.* ANNABELLE *slowly turns to* MRS. WALWORTH. *She smiles as she sees that* MRS. WALWORTH *understands, then she rises and closes and locks the steel door. She closes the louvered doors.*)

MRS. WALWORTH

(*Takes cigarette case from purse. Polishing fingerprints from it*)
Of course, my dear, I shall have to raise my rates. Double at least, I should think. That would be eighty dollars the week.
(*She puts the case on the coffee table and sits.* ANNA-BELLE *opens the hall doors.*)

ANNABELLE

(Going to bell pull)

I should like some tea. . . . *(Pulls cord)* A nice cup of tea. . . .

Curtain

ACT TWO

ACT TWO

Scene 1

The Library. The following Friday, shortly before noon. At rise, the stage is empty. ANNABELLE *enters quickly from balcony, conscious that someone is approaching from terrace. She goes directly to the desk, takes a pair of scissors from the pocket of her apron. She is about to put the scissors in the sheath when she notices a thread caught in the blades. She disentangles it, puts the scissors in the sheath, and puts the sheath in a desk drawer. She busies herself with papers on the desk as* CONNIE *enters from terrace.*

ANNABELLE

Connie, dear! Where's Janie? Didn't she go walking with you?

CONNIE

Yes . . . she's watching Ricky work on his boat.

ANNABELLE

(*Picking up newspaper*)
Come see this! On the front page, just as they promised. I'm so pleased!

CONNIE

(*Takes paper*)

Well . . . look at me! I owe the Visiting Nurses an apology . . . and a large contribution.

ANNABELLE

It's a beautiful picture of you . . . and thank you so much. Connie, Doctor Lindstrum phoned while you were out.

CONNIE

Oh, yes.

ANNABELLE

I hope you didn't mind my sending Joe to the vet's?

CONNIE

No, of course not. I want to know what happened.

ANNABELLE

Well, he says there are no broken bones, no marks at all. He couldn't have been hit by a car or killed in a fight with another dog. He asked me if there was any likelihood of his being poisoned. I told him we'd considered that and we couldn't believe it possible. Anyway, he's going to perform an autopsy. I said it was all right. I hope you agree.

CONNIE

(*Turning away*)

Yes . . . (*She goes to sofa, sits*) It's a beautiful day, isn't it?

64

ANNABELLE

Yes . . . Connie, are you planning on taking your green dress to Pawling on Saturday?

CONNIE

I thought I would.

ANNABELLE

Fine. I'll have it pressed and that will be done and out of the way.

(*She pulls the bell cord.*)

CONNIE

(*Laughing, but annoyed*)

Annabelle, I can take care of my own clothes! I can ask Mildred to press my dress.

ANNABELLE

I enjoy it. I hope Charles won't be later than he thought. I've ordered an early lunch.

(MILDRED *enters from hall.*)

MILDRED

Yes, Ma'am?

ANNABELLE

Mildred, will you press Mrs. Ashton's green dress. . . .

CONNIE

Don't bother, Mildred. It's silly to press it, then pack it. . . .

ANNABELLE

Mildred packs beautifully. There won't be a wrinkle in it.
(*To* MILDRED) I've laid it out on Mrs. Ashton's bed.
(MILDRED *hesitates.*)

CONNIE

Very well, Mildred.

MILDRED

Yes, Ma'am.
(*She exits.*)

ANNABELLE

Do you still intend to take the four-eighteen?

CONNIE

The four-eighteen, yes.

ANNABELLE

Then you will have time for some shopping . . . and I
wanted to remind you . . . do look at those wonderful cash-
meres at Saks. You'll find I'm not being a bit overenthusiastic
about them.

CONNIE

I don't know about shopping . . . I thought I'd stop in
and see Betsy McLane.

ANNABELLE

(*Casually*)

Oh, really? I gathered you were so looking forward to an
hour's shopping.

CONNIE

No, I thought I'd have Betsy calm me down about this television thing.

ANNABELLE

Connie! You're not nervous about it!

CONNIE

Well, let's say I'm uneasy. I'd like Betsy to brief me. She's an old hand at quiz shows.

ANNABELLE

Does she know you're coming, dear? Is she expecting you?

CONNIE

No, and I won't bother calling her. I'll just drop in. She'll be home resting for her performance tonight.

(MILDRED *steps onto the balcony. She carries the green dress; she is upset.*)

MILDRED

(*Urgently*)

Miss Annabelle . . .

ANNABELLE

Mildred, for Heaven's sake, what is it?

MILDRED

(*Coming downstairs*)

Something terrible . . .

67

CONNIE

What is it? The children!

MILDRED

Oh, no, Mrs. Ashton! It's this dress, your dress. . . .

CONNIE

(*Relieved*)
Mildred! If it's only my dress . . .

MILDRED

Mrs. Ashton . . . look! (*She holds up the dress*) It's
been ruined! It's in shreds!

CONNIE

What happened to it?

MILDRED

It wasn't an accident, it was on purpose. Look! It's been
cut . . . slashed with a knife or something.

CONNIE

Slashed with a knife . . . but who? . . .
(*A pause.*)

ANNABELLE

What on earth—

MILDRED

(*Reluctantly*)
Ricky . . . it must have been Ricky. . . .
(CHARLES *enters from terrace. He carries a roll of
blueprints, puts them on the desk*.)

68

CONNIE

No, he wouldn't . . . Ricky couldn't do a thing like that!

CHARLES

Ricky couldn't do a thing like what? What's going on?

ANNABELLE

Connie's dress, Charles . . . Show it to him, Mildred.

MILDRED

(*Holds up dress*)
It's all cut . . . ruined. . . .

CHARLES

(*Goes to* MILDRED, *looks at dress*)
Ricky couldn't have done that.

CONNIE

No!

MILDRED

It must have been him, Mr. Ashton.

CHARLES

Why should he? Where was the dress?

ANNABELLE

On Connie's bed. I laid it out just after Connie and Janie went for a walk. That was about eleven.

69

CHARLES

Has Ricky been upstairs since then?

ANNABELLE

He might have been, I don't know.

CHARLES

Mildred, do you know?

MILDRED

Yes, he was. He didn't go down to his boat till a little while ago.

ANNABELLE

(*Quietly, as though she hates saying it*)
Yes, Mildred's right, I'm afraid. I remember . . . Ricky was upstairs when I laid out the dress.

CHARLES

Mildred, will you ask Ricky to come here? (*She hesitates*) Just say that I want to see him.

MILDRED

Yes, sir.
(*She exits out to terrace.*)

CONNIE

(*Miserably*)
The poor kid. . . . Darling, he couldn't have realized . . .

ANNABELLE

Yes, Charles, let's not exaggerate this.

CHARLES

(*Impatiently*)

I'm not exaggerating anything! I'm not going to horse-whip the kid . . . I'm going to *talk* to him.

ANNABELLE

But listen to me, please. You see, I think I know exactly why Ricky did this. He wanted to go to the carnival tomor-row . . . you know that. He had his heart set on seeing the Death Defying Leap. Now don't you see? He must have thought that by ruining Connie's dress it would pre-vent you from going to Pawling tomorrow. And you'd take him to the carnival instead.

CONNIE

I never realized that it meant so much to him! Charles, how stupid of us! We could have gone to Pawling later . . .

CHARLES

Sure we could. But at the moment that isn't the point. When a nine-year-old boy can take a knife and do what he did! Because he wants to go to a carnival . . .

(MILDRED *enters from terrace*.)

MILDRED

Here he is, Mr. Ashton.

CHARLES

Thank you, Mildred.

MILDRED

(*Calls out to terrace*)

Come on in, Ricky.

(*She exits.* RICKY *enters slowly. He is uncertain, a little frightened. He comes to the center of the room, though, and stands directly in front of* CHARLES. *He looks at him quizzically.*)

CHARLES

Do you know why I wanted to see you, Ricky?

RICKY

No, Mildred just said you did.

CHARLES

You seem . . . a little worried.

RICKY

Mildred said you wanted to see me this minute. When she says "this minute" I know it's nothing good.

CHARLES

Look, Rick, it isn't good. (*Holds up dress*) This is Connie's dress. You see what happened to it?

RICKY

It's all torn.

CHARLES

It was slashed with a knife.
> (RICKY *knows he's going to be blamed for it. He becomes tense, frightened.*)

RICKY

I didn't do anything!

CHARLES

Ricky, you knew Connie was going to wear that dress tomorrow, didn't you? And you want to go to the carnival tomorrow instead of today. . . .

RICKY

I didn't tear her dress!

CHARLES

No one else could have done it. . . .

RICKY

I didn't! I didn't go near her old dress!

CHARLES

> (*Puts dress on desk. Puts his hands on* RICKY's *shoulders and speaks gently to him*)

Ricky, sometimes people want things so badly . . . they go about getting them in the wrong way. They get mad

73

and mixed up and they do things . . . things they'd give their right arm not to have done, but it's too late. Then the only thing they can do is to tell the truth and say they're sorry . . .

RICKY

But I'm not sorry! I didn't do it. . . .

CHARLES

We know you did. . . . I'm going to have to punish you.

RICKY

Go ahead, punish me. I don't care. . . . How are you going to punish me? Stay in my room? I can't work on my boat?

CHARLES

Nothing that easy. I'm sorry. Something more than that.

RICKY

(*Quietly, bitterly*)
I didn't do it. I didn't touch her . . .

CHARLES

Go to your room, Ricky.

RICKY

I never even saw . . .

74

CHARLES

Go to your room!

RICKY

Yes, sir!
(*He runs angrily up the stairs and out the balcony door.*)

CHARLES

(*Going to* CONNIE)
Darling, Ricky didn't do this to you . . . he doesn't feel that way about you . . .

CONNIE

I hope not . . . I hope not . . .

CHARLES

It was his way of getting to see the Death Defying Leap tomorrow. . . .

ANNABELLE

Charles, perhaps he shouldn't go to the carnival at all.

CHARLES

Maybe you're right.

CONNIE

Darling . . .

CHARLES

(*To* CONNIE)

He's got to be punished. Maybe this is what he needs, maybe we've been too lenient with him.

(JANIE *enters on balcony and comes downstairs.*)

JANIE

What's wrong with Ricky? He won't talk to me, he slammed the door.

ANNABELLE

He's been a naughty boy, dear . . . never mind . . .

JANIE

What did he do?

CHARLES

Don't worry about it, Janie.

ANNABELLE

You worry about lunch. It's almost ready. Off you go!

JANIE

(*Going to hall doors*)

What are we having?

ANNABELLE

Wait and be surprised. Darlings, do go in. (CONNIE *and* CHARLES *start out*) Oh, Charles, Connie's taking the four-eighteen and I'll be getting back from Mrs. Walworth's by then. Yes, that will be all right.

CHARLES

What will be all right?

ANNABELLE

I don't want Ricky to be left alone.

CONNIE

Alone?

ANNABELLE

Yes, you see, I've given the servants the afternoon off. So they can go to the carnival, too. There'll be no one here this afternoon but you and Ricky. Have a nice lunch.

JANIE

Come on, Daddy. . . .
(*She takes* CHARLES's *hand and they exit.*)

ANNABELLE

Oh, Connie! It will be all right . . . I'm sure . . .

CONNIE

(*Grimly, but smiling*)
Thank you, Annabelle.
(*She exits.* ANNABELLE *goes to the desk, picks up the dress, smiling, pleased. She starts for the stairs with it.* MRS. WALWORTH *appears at terrace door. She is carrying a large bunch of purple gladiolas.*)

77

MRS. WALWORTH

(*Whispering*)

My dear!

ANNABELLE

(*Startled, whirls toward her, throwing dress onto chair*)
What are you doing here?

MRS. WALWORTH

Annabelle, my dear . . .

ANNABELLE

Does anyone know you've come? Did anyone see you?

MRS. WALWORTH

Not a soul, but it doesn't matter. I've changed my mind.
(ANNABELLE *goes quickly out hall doors and closes them*) Yes,
I have. You're not to go through with it.

ANNABELLE

(*Facing her*)

Sit down . . . . be quiet, let me think! (*She snatches
the gladiolas from* MRS. WALWORTH) The glads are all
that matter. I can explain your being here, but if anyone
saw the glads . . . You're positive no one saw you?

MRS. WALWORTH

Quite. There's no one at all about. But you needn't
concern yourself . . .

ANNABELLE

Please be quiet . . . just be quiet (ANNABELLE *goes with the gladiolas to cupboard in bookshelves, opens top cupboard, puts the glads in it, closes it, locks it, and puts key in her pocket. She comes back to* MRS. WALWORTH) You've been drinking, haven't you?

MRS. WALWORTH

A drop to steady my nerves.

ANNABELLE

More than a drop. I can see that. Much more than a drop. On the day I needed you most.

MRS. WALWORTH

You don't listen. I've decided not to let you do it.

ANNABELLE

As though you could stop me!

MRS. WALWORTH

Oh, I can stop you easily enough. (*Takes letter from purse and waves it in front of* ANNABELLE) With our little Lucinda's help.

ANNABELLE

(*Quietly now; gently*)
Mrs. Walworth, has something happened? What's made you change your mind? I assure you, there's no need at all to be nervous.

(MRS. WALWORTH *returns the letter to her purse.*)

79

MRS. WALWORTH

Something might go wrong.

ANNABELLE

Everything is going splendidly. I can't imagine what is upsetting you.

MRS. WALWORTH

I don't know . . . so many things . . .

ANNABELLE

(*Seating* MRS. WALWORTH *on sofa, sits beside her*)
If you could be more definite?

MRS. WALWORTH

Well . . . the vault. Yes, the vault.

ANNABELLE

Now, just what about the vault?

MRS. WALWORTH

The dog . . . did it really suffocate? It might have killed itself somehow trying to get out.

ANNABELLE

The vault is quite airtight. Of course, the poor little dog was in a frenzy. It took about an hour for the dog. It will take two for her.

MRS. WALWORTH

You seem so certain of that.

80

ANNABELLE

Oh, yes, I made certain of it. It was rather a frightening experience, I must say.

MRS. WALWORTH

You put yourself in the vault?

ANNABELLE

Yes! The first hour and a half was most uncomfortable. Then it began to get oppressive. In about an hour and three-quarters, I was gasping and I almost blacked out. Another few minutes would have surely done me in. So you see, I am quite certain. Two hours.

MRS. WALWORTH

She's a bit younger and quicker than you . . .

ANNABELLE

Don't let that concern you. They're all at lunch now. Everyone will be gone by three . . . except the two of them, of course. By three-thirty . . . (*She rises*) . . . I should have her in there. No one will be getting back much before half-past five, and by that time . . . Two hours . . . that will have done it.

MRS. WALWORTH

I don't know. That seems to be cutting it rather close to me.

ANNABELLE

No, actually, it will all be over by five-thirty. But even then she won't be missed till after eight. That's when she's due at the television studio. I expect the television people will phone a bit after eight. And it might take hours . . . before anyone realizes where she is.

MRS. WALWORTH

Aren't you worried that she may not co-operate and go into the vault?

ANNABELLE

Dear, please give me credit for a little intelligence. She'll go into the vault.

MRS. WALWORTH

Yes, but once you've slammed the door and locked it . . . well, it occurs to me that if I were in her shoes, I'd do a great deal of screaming.

ANNABELLE

You would, yes, but she won't. She'll realize it's quite useless . . . nobody would hear her. She'll keep her head.

MRS. WALWORTH

But she just might scream, and somebody might hear her.

ANNABELLE

Did you hear the dog barking? You were here in the room at the time. Did you hear the dog?

MRS. WALWORTH

No.

ANNABELLE

There you are.

MRS. WALWORTH

How do I know it was barking?

ANNABELLE

What, my dear?

MRS. WALWORTH

If I couldn't hear it bark, how could I possibly know if it was barking or not?

ANNABELLE

I do wish you wouldn't drink.

MRS. WALWORTH

Did you hear it bark?

ANNABELLE

No, of course not!

MRS. WALWORTH

Well!

83

ANNABELLE

(*Goes to vault, throws open louvered doors*)
Come here! Come and look at the thickness of the door
and walls. (*She works combination, throws open the steel
door*) There you are!

MRS. WALWORTH

(*Peering into vault*)
Gloomy, isn't it! And so small! Not the least bit inviting.

ANNABELLE

No, but if you like I'll go in and close the door and
scream my head off. You won't hear a sound.

MRS. WALWORTH

Now, don't be silly, Annabelle. I couldn't possibly trust
you. I'm sure you wouldn't bother to open your mouth.

ANNABELLE

I'd promise.

MRS. WALWORTH

No. So long as I lived I'd never know if you had screamed
or not.

ANNABELLE

Very well. You go in, and you scream.

84

MRS. WALWORTH

(*Looks at* ANNABELLE *a moment, starts into vault then stops and steps quickly away from it*)

No. No, really, let's not even consider that. I'm not going to give you the opportunity of saving forty a week.

ANNABELLE

(*Closes vault door, then louvered door*)

At the moment, you're completely indispensable to me.

MRS. WALWORTH

Why, yes, I am, aren't I? Your alibi. Yes, you must keep me safe and sound, mustn't you? Come to think of it, I haven't enjoyed such a sense of security in your presence for quite some time. Still . . . (*She glances at vault*) I much prefer being on this side of that door.

ANNABELLE

Then you'll just have to take my word for it. Now are you quite happy about everything?

MRS. WALWORTH

I'm encouraged . . . Yes, you've been most encouraging. But I should like to think a little . . .

ANNABELLE

I'm afraid there's hardly time for that. You know, I *have* agreed that it would mean eighty a week for you, and perhaps a bit more.

MRS. WALWORTH

I must say that is tempting. . . .
(CONNIE *is heard in the hall.* ANNABELLE *goes quickly to the desk,* MRS. WALWORTH *to the sofa.* CONNIE *enters.*)

ANNABELLE

Did you have a nice lunch, Connie?

CONNIE

Very nice. Hello, Mrs. Walworth.

MRS. WALWORTH

My dear, how are you?

ANNABELLE

Mrs. Walworth is just leaving. She was in the neighborhood and stopped in to make sure I was coming for tea this afternoon . . .

MRS. WALWORTH

(*Picking up purse from coffee table*)
And I'm so glad you can, Annabelle. Come as early as you can . . . I do get so lonely.

ANNABELLE

You poor thing! I'll be there shortly after three.
(MRS. WALWORTH *turns and looks at* CONNIE.)

MRS. WALWORTH

I don't believe I've told you . . . and I do want you to know. I've enjoyed your pictures so much, so very much. (*She looks at* ANNABELLE, *then back to* CONNIE) Goodbye, my dear.

(*She exits.*)

Curtain

Scene 2

The Library. Later the same afternoon.
At rise, CHARLES *is standing in the terrace doorway.*
ANNABELLE *enters from balcony door. She has changed from
her house dress to tweeds and walking shoes.*

CHARLES

(Calling)

Janie! Janie . . . hurry up, baby!

ANNABELLE

(Coming downstairs)

Oh, you've found her?

CHARLES

(Turning to her)

Yes, I did.

ANNABELLE

Good. I almost wish I were going with you.

CHARLES

You're invited.

ANNABELLE

No, Mrs. Walworth is expecting me. I mustn't disappoint
her . . . and then I've promised Connie I'd bring her
back some gladiolas.

(JANIE *runs in.*)

JANIE

Is it time to go?

CHARLES

It's time for you to get ready to go. Connie's waiting to
get you started.

JANIE

I wish Ricky was going. Can't he, please?

CHARLES

No, baby.

JANIE

It'd be more fun.

CHARLES

You and I will have fun. (*Slaps her on her bottom*)
On your horse, sweetheart.

(*She starts for the stairs.* ANNABELLE *stops her by
putting arm around her.*)

89

ANNABELLE

You'll have a lovely time, Janie. It's a gorgeous afternoon and the carnival's always so very gay. Charles, why
don't you take some color pictures?

JANIE

(*Running upstairs*)

Yes, Daddy! Then Ricky can at least see some pictures
of it. . . .

(JANIE *exits*.)

CHARLES

I think I will take some pictures! (*Starts for hall*) There
should still be film in the camera.

(*He stops in hall.*)

ANNABELLE

(*Turning to him*)

What is it?

CHARLES

(*Going to cupboard*)

I just remembered. . . . The camera's in the cupboard here.

ANNABELLE

Oh, no, I don't think so. . . .

90

CHARLES

(*Turning knob*)

Yes, I put it in here, I remember. It's locked. Where's the key?

ANNABELLE

Isn't it there?

CHARLES

(*Looking on floor for key*)

No.

ANNABELLE

That's strange.

CHARLES

Yes, this hasn't been locked for years. Not since my father kept his bourbon in it. The bourbon that was too good for children.

(*He goes to the desk, and looks in the drawer as* MILDRED *enters from hall.*)

ANNABELLE

I don't believe your camera's in there. You do mean the big one . . . the new one? (*Sees* MILDRED) Yes, Mildred?

CHARLES

(*Turning to* MILDRED)

Oh, Mildred, have you seen the key to this cupboard?

MILDRED

No, sir. Isn't it there? It was the other day.

CHARLES

No, it's gone.
(*He exits to hall.*)

ANNABELLE

It'll turn up. Yes, Mildred, what was it? Are you leaving now?

MILDRED

Cook and I both, yes.

ANNABELLE

Do you have a ride into town?

MILDRED

(*Nodding*)
Fred's here. He's waiting.

ANNABELLE

Then you run along. Is Fred taking you to the carnival?

MILDRED

Yes, he is. (CONNIE *enters on balcony*) Well, good-bye, Miss Annabelle, and thank you for the afternoon off.

ANNABELLE

Why, don't you mention it. Just enjoy yourself.

CONNIE

(*On balcony*)

Yes, Mildred, have fun.

MILDRED

Thank you, Mrs. Ashton. Good-bye.
(*She exits.*)

CONNIE

Well, I've got Janie under control. (*She comes down the stairs*) Now where's Charles?

ANNABELLE

About some place.

CONNIE

He's not playing in the mud, I hope.

ANNABELLE

No, looking for his camera, I think. If you'll excuse me, Connie, I must make a few calls about the auction.
(*She opens the phone file as* CHARLES *enters with a screwdriver and goes directly to cupboard.* ANNABELLE *dials a number.*)

CONNIE

Charles?

CHARLES

Yes?

CONNIE

What are you doing, darling?

CHARLES

We can't find the key to the cupboard.

(ANNABELLE, *seeing* CHARLES *working on cupboard, hangs up.*)

ANNABELLE

What on earth! (*She steps to* CHARLES) Really, now!

CHARLES

It shouldn't be too hard to get this open.

ANNABELLE

But you're wasting your time! The camera isn't in there! I'm positive!

CHARLES

(*Working on lock*)

Would you like to bet on that? (*Suddenly he pulls off doorknob. Returns front, holding it up*) Hey, have you ever seen half a doorknob?

CONNIE

Darling, you're tearing down our house.

CHARLES

I've always meant to tear it down. First minute I've had.

ANNABELLE

All this trouble. Tomorrow I'll get a locksmith. . . .

CHARLES

It's no trouble. I enjoy this type of work. Breaking and entering.

ANNABELLE

(*Laughing, as though* CHARLES *were being too silly for words*)

But I tell you the camera isn't there! Connie, you remember . . . the Sunday before last . . . you and Charles went for a walk . . .

CONNIE

Yes . . .

ANNABELLE

You took the camera with you. . . . Charles, do stop and listen to me!

CHARLES

I can hear you.

ANNABELLE

You remember taking the camera with you. Of course you do!

CHARLES

(*Working on lock*)

No, I didn't take it with me.

95

ANNABELLE

Connie, you remember!

CONNIE

Yes, it seems to me he did take it.

ANNABELLE

And he didn't bring it back!

CONNIE

Well, I hadn't thought about it . . . No, I don't think he did.

ANNABELLE

(*With an eye on* CHARLES)
You stopped off somewhere . . . to see someone . . .

CONNIE

Yes, we did.

ANNABELLE

Charles might have left the camera there. Where did you stop? The Fergusons?

CONNIE

No, I don't believe that was the name . . . but then I've met so many people lately.

ANNABELLE

(*Going to* CHARLES *at cupboard*)
Charles! Was it the Fergusons?

CHARLES

(*Still at work, laughs*)

Ferguson . . . Ferguson . . . that name's familiar.

ANNABELLE

Oh, no, Charles! Please answer me. Was it the Leonards? (*To* CONNIE) Connie, the Leonards?

CONNIE

That could have been it . . . tall people, both of them . . . three kids. . . .

ANNABELLE

Yes! The Leonards! (*Goes to desk, flips open file*) I'm just going to teach you a lesson. I'm going to prove to you how very wrong you can be at times. (*Dialing*) I hope the Leonards are home. . . .

CHARLES

It doesn't matter. I'll have this opened in a minute. . . .

ANNABELLE

(*Into phone*)

Hello, Claire . . . this is Annabelle Logan. I'm fine . . . how are you?

CHARLES

She isn't talking to Claire. (*Steps to* CONNIE) She isn't talking to anyone.

97

ANNABELLE

(*Into phone*)

Did Charles leave a camera at your place a few Sundays ago? Oh, would you? (*To* CHARLES) You might as well stop. She's asking Sam.

CHARLES

(*To* CONNIE)

That proves she's bluffing. Claire hasn't spoken to Sam for twenty years.

ANNABELLE

(*Into phone*)

Yes, Claire?

CHARLES

Give me that phone (*Takes it*) Hello . . . (*Surprised*) Claire? Is that you? . . . Well, is my camera there? All right, I'll stop over and get it. See you soon.

(*He hangs up.*)

ANNABELLE

Well?

CHARLES

Okay, you can gloat.

ANNABELLE

Yes, I can and I should, but I simply haven't time. (*Heading for the stairs*) You ought to be getting off soon, too,

Charles, especially if you're going to stop for your camera
. . . which . . . is . . . at . . . the Leonards', isn't it?
(*She exits from balcony.*)

CHARLES

I was positive it was in there. I'd better put this thing
back together.

CONNIE
(*Rising*)

Darling . . .

CHARLES

Yes?

CONNIE

Take Ricky to the carnival with you!

CHARLES
(*Goes to desk, puts screwdriver down*)
Has Janie been needling you about that?

CONNIE

No, I'm asking for my sake. Take him, I want you to take
him!

CHARLES

How the hell can I . . . after what he's done!
(CHARLES *takes an envelope from the drawer, puts
knob and screws into it.*)

99

CONNIE

Darling, the way things are between Ricky and me, he shouldn't be punished now, not today!

CHARLES

(*Putting envelope into drawer and closing it*)
We can't overlook this, Connie!

CONNIE

Up till now Ricky's merely resented me . . . I hope. But now at this moment he's up in his room hating me! He's being punished because of me. He blames me for not being able to work on his boat. for having to stay in his room . . . for missing the carnival . . . Oh, darling, this isn't the way to handle it, it's much too drastic.

CHARLES

What he did was a little drastic.

CONNIE

Darling, I'm frightened about Ricky and me! I was hoping I could handle it alone . . . I was sure I could, but I'm not sure now. Somehow it's got away from me, and I need your help! Please . . . (RICKY *enters on balcony*) Oh, hello, Ricky.

CHARLES

Hiya, Rick.

RICKY

(*Coming downstairs*)

Miss Annabelle said I could work on my boat. I don't have to stay in my room any more.

(CONNIE *turns back to* CHARLES. *She touches his arm, pleading.*)

CHARLES

Rick . . .

RICKY

What?

CHARLES

Look . . . in California . . . we had a good time out there . . . you and Janie and Connie and I . . . we had a lot of fun together, didn't we? (RICKY *nods*) But here . . . something's gone wrong here. We're going to fix that and start all over as if nothing ever went wrong. But first . . . about what happened today . . . we've got to fix that first. That was a bad mistake you made . . . but lots of people make mistakes . . . Why, people make so many mistakes, they should have rubber heads like pencils . . . You know, erasers, so they can correct their own mistakes.

RICKY

(*Not smiling*)

Yes, sir.

CHARLES

So you make a mistake today. That was too bad. But it's even worse not to tell the truth, not to admit your mistake and apologize. You're being kept at home today . . . not just because of what you did to Connie's dress, but because you didn't tell the truth. Now, if you'll admit it and tell Connie you're sorry . . . you can go to the carnival.

(*A pause before* RICKY *speaks.* ANNABELLE *appears on balcony. She listens, unseen.*)

RICKY

You mean . . . all I have to do is say I ripped her dress and tell her I'm sorry?

CHARLES

Yes. And I'll take you with us this afternoon . . . and somehow I'll make sure that tomorrow you see the Death Defying Leap into the Pool of Fire!

RICKY

(*Agonized*)

Gee . . .

CONNIE

Ricky, you needn't apologize to me. . . . We want you to go to the carnival.

RICKY

(*Turns front, speaks very quietly*)

Okay . . . I cut up your dress. . . .

CHARLES

What did you say, Rick?

RICKY

I cut up her dress.

CONNIE

(*Going to* RICKY)

Ricky, it's all right now . . . it's all over. Nothing ever happened. You go to the carnival and have a wonderful time. That was a brave thing you just did. You've earned yourself a wonderful time.

(*She rumples his hair. He pulls back from her.*)

RICKY

Don't touch me!

(CONNIE *is stunned.*)

CHARLES

(*His shock explodes in anger*)

Ricky!

RICKY

I don't care! I didn't tear her old dress! I never even saw her old dress! (*Starts running toward terrace*) I don't want to go to the damn carnival!

(*He runs out.* CHARLES *starts to follow him.*)

103

CHARLES

Ricky, come back here. . . .

CONNIE

No, Charles . . . not now. . . .

> (ANNABELLE *steps back out of sight in balcony doorway as* CHARLES *turns to* CONNIE. *There is a slight pause.*)

ANNABELLE

(*Offstage, on balcony*)

Janie! Janie, dear, hurry! Daddy's waiting for you. (ANNABELLE *enters, starts downstairs*) Well, I'm off to Mrs. Walworth's. Oh, Charles, I've told Ricky he might play with his boat.

CHARLES

(*Turning to* ANNABELLE)

Yes, I know.

ANNABELLE

I thought it was going a bit too far to keep the child indoors on such a delightful day. Connie, it's much too nice to have to go to New York . . . but then, I suppose you will have fun. I'll be watching your show tonight, darling. Don't be nervous.

CONNIE

Thank you, Annabelle.

ANNABELLE

'Bye, 'bye, dears.
    (*She exits through hall as* JANIE *enters on balcony.*
CONNIE *turns to* JANIE *on stairs.*)

CONNIE

Oh, there you are, Janie. Why, you look pretty enough to go to a carnival.

JANIE

I am going to a carnival.

CONNIE

I know you are.

JANIE

Let's go, Daddy.

CHARLES

Yes, darling. You wait in the car for me, I'll be right out.

JANIE

Okay.

CONNIE

Have a good time, sweetie.

JANIE

Thank you, 'bye.
    (*She exits to terrace.*)

CHARLES

Connie . . .

CONNIE

Darling, thank you for trying . . .
(*He takes her in his arms.*)

CHARLES

Look, you go to New York and take a little vacation from the Ashton family. You deserve it.

CONNIE

No. I wish I hadn't promised to do this silly television thing. I'll hurry back.
(*They kiss.*)

JANIE

(*Offstage*)

Come on, Daddy!
(CHARLES *releases* CONNIE *and exits.* CONNIE *follows him to door, stands watching for a moment, then turns back. She pauses for a moment before she goes and looks at the clock, then exits upstairs. The clock strikes three. The stage is empty for a few moments, then* CONNIE *reappears on balcony with her purse. She comes down the stairs to the sofa and puts her purse on the coffee table. She takes a cigarette case from the purse and begins to fill it from the cigarette box on the coffee table. The phone rings. She answers it.*)

CONNIE

Hello . . . no, this is Mrs. Ashton . . . oh, yes, Mrs. Weaver, we met the other day . . . the picture. Why, thank you . . . I hope the auction's a big success. Annabelle just left a moment ago. She went over to Mrs. Walworth's . . . she'll be back about four-thirty . . . would you like her to call you? Oh . . . all right, good-bye, Mrs. Weaver. (*She hangs up and goes back to coffee table, finishes filling cigarette case, puts it in purse, picks up script and is putting it in purse when she hears a noise upstairs*) Ricky? (*She starts up to the balcony.* RICKY *appears in terrace doorway.* CONNIE *sees him*) Oh . . . hi.

RICKY

Are you busy?

CONNIE

No, you wanted to talk to me?

RICKY

Yes . . . (*Now he's a little timid*) But if you're busy, I can come back later.

CONNIE

No, stick around, talk to me. (*Her attitude is consciously casual*) Everybody's gone but us.

RICKY

(*Goes to* CONNIE, *pulling a bankbook in its envelope from his back pocket. He thrusts it into* CONNIE'*s hands*)
Here, take it.

CONNIE

(*Reads*)

"The First National Bank and Trust Company." (*Takes bankbook out of its envelope*) "In account with Richard Wells Ashton . . ."

RICKY

(*Matter of fact*)

Wells . . . that was my mother's name before it was Ashton. Elizabeth Wells.

CONNIE

Yes, I know. (*Looks at book*) "One hundred and eighteen dollars and seventy-two cents."

RICKY

It's mine. I can do whatever I want with it.

CONNIE

I'm sure you can. Did you earn it?

RICKY

Part of it. I want you to use it. To buy a ticket to California.

CONNIE

Oh.

RICKY

It's enough, isn't it?

108

CONNIE

Yes . . .

RICKY

How soon can you get ready?

CONNIE

Pretty quickly. I guess you'd help me pack, wouldn't you?

RICKY

I couldn't help you much. I'm not allowed in your room. I'm never to go in it again.

CONNIE

Who said so?

RICKY

Miss Annabelle. I'm allowed to go any place I want in the whole house except your room. Are you going back to California? To Hollywood?

CONNIE

I guess I'd better, Rick.

RICKY

You could sleep in California.

CONNIE

(*Puzzled; smiles*)

I'm sleeping all right here.

RICKY

I mean in the mornings. You could sleep till noon. You wouldn't be able to hear me in California.

CONNIE

Hear you?

RICKY

Make so much noise. I know actresses aren't like other people.

CONNIE

Miss Annabelle tell you that?

RICKY

(*Nods*)

It isn't your fault. You aren't used to children.

CONNIE

(*A laugh*)

Ricky . . . (*Sits on sofa*) When I was working in a picture, which in the past twelve years has been almost always, I got up at five o'clock in the morning.

RICKY

Then you must be tired. And I keep you awake.

CONNIE

(*Laughs*)

I'm not tired. Do I look tired?

RICKY

No. (*A simple statement, not flattery*) You look pretty good. I always liked you in the movies.

CONNIE

It's just around the house, huh?

RICKY

Aren't you kind of anxious to get back? (*Indicates bankbook*) You can use that till you get a job again. You will be able to get a job, won't you?

CONNIE

I guess so. But—don't worry about it. And I'll **pay you** back out of my first week's salary.

RICKY

It isn't a loan. I'm giving it to you.

CONNIE

Well, thanks again.

RICKY

(*Gravely*)

Don't mention it. It's a pleasure. When will you be going?

CONNIE

Well, let's see . . . I've got this television thing tonight . . .

RICKY

Daddy said Janie and I could stay up to see you.

CONNIE

Oh, I don't know if it'll be worth it. You won't get to bed till ten o'clock. Of course, if you want to sleep in the morning, I'll be real quiet.

RICKY

(*Smiles*)

Nobody can wake me up.

CONNIE

I know! Nine-year-old boys aren't like other people.

RICKY

(*Coming to sofa, slowly*)

I want to see you tonight. I saw you once before on television. A movie. You shot Richard Widmark.

CONNIE

Sorry about that. But he had it coming to him.

RICKY

Sure! He was asking for it!

CONNIE

Askin' for it? He was beggin' for it! The double-crossin' rat!

112

RICKY

(*Sits beside her on sofa*)

How many times did you shoot him?

CONNIE

As I recall, I emptied my gun into him.

RICKY

That would be six times. You only had one gun, didn't you?

CONNIE

Yes. Cheap picture. You do like movies, don't you?

RICKY

Some of them. I like sailing more than anything.

CONNIE

I like sailing. Fun.

RICKY

Do you like baseball? I do. Do you?

CONNIE

No.

RICKY

Oh. I think it's pretty good.

CONNIE

I don't like base, basket or volley ball.

RICKY

Do you like foot?

CONNIE

High school, college or professional foot?

RICKY

Well, high school, for instance.

CONNIE

Oh . . . it's okay.

RICKY

College?

CONNIE

Oh . . . it's okay.

RICKY

Professional?

CONNIE

Professional American or professional Canadian?

RICKY

Well, professional American.

CONNIE

Which league?

RICKY

There's only one.

CONNIE

There is not! There are two leagues! Just like big league baseball.

RICKY

No. One league with two divisions.

CONNIE

How much do you want to bet?

RICKY

(*Picks up bankbook from sofa*)
A hundred and eighteen dollars and seventy-two cents!

CONNIE

Say, listen, how would you like to go to New York with me?

RICKY

When?

CONNIE

Now! Right away! We've got a lot to talk about. You know, this is the first time we've ever been alone together for more than a minute.

RICKY

You mean I could go to the television studio with you?

CONNIE

Sure. You want to?

RICKY

(*Rising*)

Yes! (*Then shakes his head*) No, I'd be in your way.

CONNIE

If you're in the way, I'll tell you to move over. (*She rises*)
Let's take an earlier train. How long will it take you to get
ready? A half-hour? Can we make the three forty-five?

RICKY

Easy, sure, but . . .

CONNIE

What?

RICKY

I'm not supposed to go anywhere! Listen, I didn't tear
your dress!

CONNIE

Of course you didn't. Let's not even think about that any
more. We'll leave a note for your father. We can see a movie
. . . maybe even Radio City . . . and we'll still have lots

of time for dinner. Any restaurant in town, you name it! Where would you like to eat?

> RICKY

Chock Full o' Nuts.

> CONNIE

All right. Let's get moving.

> RICKY

I have to fix my paint cans.

> CONNIE

Hurry up. (*Starts him toward terrace*) I'll call a cab.
(*As* RICKY *dashes out,* CONNIE *goes to the phone. She is starting to dial when she hears* RICKY.)

> RICKY

> (*Offstage*)

Hey, Connie! (CONNIE *hangs up phone and hides behind chair.* RICKY *enters*) Hey, Connie!

> CONNIE

> (*Rising from behind chair*)

Lissen, pardner . . .

> RICKY

> (*Wheeling to her, laughing*)

Hey!

CONNIE

Never turn your back on an overstuffed chair.

RICKY

Okay.

CONNIE

What are you doing here? What about your paint cans?

RICKY

Do I have to take a bath?

CONNIE

I'd say so. It might take you all of two minutes. What did you have in mind?

RICKY

Well . . . I need one, but on second thought . . . You going to take one?

CONNIE

I've had mine. I felt as though I should. You know, television. I'm going to be invited into millions of living rooms.

RICKY

Okay, what the hell, I'll take one, too! And should I wear my good clothes?

CONNIE

Well, I am. In fact, since this is our first date, I'm going to wear my very best clothes.

RICKY

Okay. So will I!

CONNIE

Okay! (*They shake hands*) Well, get going!
(*He runs upstairs to balcony and exits.* CONNIE *goes
to the phone, dials. The line is busy. She hangs up,
takes a piece of paper and starts to write a note.* ANNA-
BELLE *enters from hall. She has* CONNIE's *fur coat
over her arm.*)

ANNABELLE

Connie, dear . . .

CONNIE

(*Turning quickly*)
Annabelle! . . . You scared me! You're not back from
Mrs. Walworth's already?

ANNABELLE

Such a silly thing. So clumsy of me. I twisted my ankle.

CONNIE

Oh, I'm sorry. Shouldn't you lie down or . . .

ANNABELLE

No, no, it's not as bad as all that. It's such a long walk,
though, I was afraid to risk it. So, I turned back. I thought

we'd put your furs away now. We've procrastinated long enough.

(*She puts fur coat over the back of the chair.*)

CONNIE

Thanks, Annabelle, that's nice of you. (*She is writing again*) I'm leaving a note for Charles. I'm taking Ricky into New York with me.

(ANNABELLE, *on her way to the vault, stops, turns back.*)

ANNABELLE

Taking him with you! Why, how can you? He's being punished! You know that.

(*She closes the hall doors, and goes to the vault.*)

CONNIE

I'm in a rush now, I'll explain later. I know you'll understand . . .

(ANNABELLE *opens the louvered doors, dials the combination, and opens the steel door. She turns to* CONNIE.)

ANNABELLE

Connie, dear, do put your furs away. Such lovely furs . . . you shouldn't be careless of them.

CONNIE

(*Finishing note*)

I really must hurry, Annabelle. We want to catch the train and I have to finish dressing. I wonder, would you mind doing it for me?

ANNABELLE

(*Goes to chair, picks up fur coat*)

Why, of course not.

CONNIE

It's dreadful of me to impose on you this way, I know. . . .
(CONNIE *is on her way to hall.* ANNABELLE *has picked up the fur coat and is starting to the vault just a step behind* CONNIE. *As* CONNIE *reaches the hall door,* ANNABELLE *pretends to turn her ankle. She stumbles and falls.*)

ANNABELLE

(*As she falls, utters a sharp cry*)

Connie . . .

CONNIE

(*Turns quickly to* ANNABELLE)

Annabelle . . .

ANNABELLE

My ankle . . . I can't move . . .

CONNIE

I'm sorry . . .

ANNABELLE

Take this, put it in the vault!

CONNIE

Let me help you up.

ANNABELLE

(*Vehemently*)

Put it in the vault . . . don't worry about me. I'll be all right in a minute. Don't fuss!

CONNIE

(*Takes fur coat*)

Of course. I'm sorry.

(CONNIE *steps into vault with the fur coat.* ANNA-
BELLE *springs to her feet and slams shut the steel
door cutting off* CONNIE's *scream.* ANNABELLE *quickly
closes the louvered doors.*)

RICKY

(*Offstage, upstairs*)

Hey, Connie. (ANNABELLE *hesitates a moment, then steps
out the hall doors and out of sight as* RICKY *enters through
the balcony door*) Connie! (*He stands for a moment on the
balcony and then comes down the stairs. At foot of steps he
pauses a moment*) I know you're hiding. (*Looks behind
an armchair, then behind desk. Runs out into hall, disap-
pears, taking the direction opposite* ANNABELLE's.) Hey, Connie, we'll miss our train. (*After a moment,* ANNABELLE

122

enters. She goes directly to desk and gets CONNIE's *note, crumples it and starts out to terrace doors, remembers, turns and goes to coffee table and gets* CONNIE's *purse, turns and exits through terrace doors.* RICKY *continues calling, off-stage*) Connie! (*He enters from hall*) Hey, Connie, where are you? (*Looks around the room, slowly goes to a chair and sinks disgustedly into it*) Damn women!

Curtain

ACT THREE

ACT THREE

The Library. The same afternoon. Five o'clock.

At rise, the room is empty. Most of the purple gladiolas are in a vase on the coffee table; several of them are on the coffee table, ready to be placed in a vase. There is some fern near the vase. ANNABELLE *enters from the hall wearing a housecoat. The clock strikes five. She stops, standing still until the clock strike finishes, then she turns slowly to the vault. She looks at it for a moment, then she goes to the desk, gets scissors from sheath and moves to the coffee table. She picks up a piece of fern, and snips it for arranging it with the gladiolas. She places it in the metal vase, then picks up another fern. She sits on the sofa, continuing to arrange the flowers as* JANIE *enters from the hall.*

JANIE

Hello, we're home.
> (*She has a pinwheel and a gas-filled balloon on a light string.*)

ANNABELLE

Hello there. Where's your father?

JANIE

Putting the car away.

ANNABELLE

You're back so soon!

JANIE

I got sick at my stomach. I ate too much popcorn.

ANNABELLE

Oh, Janie! Perhaps you should lie down for a little.

JANIE

I'm all right now.

ANNABELLE

Well, be quiet a while, dear. Tell me, what did you like best about the carnival?

JANIE

The popcorn.

ANNABELLE

(*Laughs*)

You are loyal, aren't you? Did your father take lots and lots of pictures?

JANIE

He let me take some, too. We took pictures of everything!

128

ANNABELLE

Then you did have some fun.

JANIE

Oh, yes!

ANNABELLE

Thank you, Miss Annabelle.

JANIE

Oh, yes! Thank you, Miss Annabelle.
(CHARLES *enters from terrace*.)

ANNABELLE

Hello, Charles! You didn't have too much popcorn, did you?

CHARLES

No, I didn't, but . . . (*Laughing, indicates* JANIE) that one, there . . .

ANNABELLE

Yes.

CHARLES

Where's Ricky? I've been looking for him. He isn't down at the pond.

ANNABELLE

He's up in his room. He'll be down in a minute, I'm sure.

CHARLES

How is he?

ANNABELLE

He's being a brave little boy. (JANIE *sits on steps*) Would you like a drink?

CHARLES

I don't think so. Did those blueprints come back from the printers yet?

ANNABELLE

Just a bit ago. They're on the hall table.
(CHARLES *gets the sketches from the hall table.*)

CHARLES

Good. I want to take them to Pawling tomorrow. Connie get off all right?
(*He comes back to the desk, sits.*)

ANNABELLE

I imagine. She'd left by the time I got back from Mrs. Walworth's.

CHARLES

You have a good time?

ANNABELLE

Yes. She's such an amusing person, Mrs. Walworth is.

CHARLES

You're going to miss her when you're in London.

ANNABELLE

I shall. You know I shall.

CHARLES

(*Picking up letter from desk*)

What's this? Doctor Lindstrom . . . the report on Connie's dog. (*Reads slowly*) The dog was suffocated . . . (*To* ANNABELLE) Suffocated? How could that have happened?

(JANIE *rises and goes to the vault.*)

ANNABELLE

I don't understand it. (*At vault,* JANIE *ties her balloon to a handle of the louvered door.* ANNABELLE *puts finishing touches on gladiolas, rises*) There. Aren't they lovely? (JANIE *starts up the stairs.* ANNABELLE *picks up vase of flowers and puts them on the end table near the sofa. Suddenly she sees the balloon*) Janie!

JANIE

(*On balcony*)

I'm going to give Ricky my pinwheel.

ANNABELLE

(*Her composure regained*)

That's my good generous girl.

JANIE

It makes me dizzy.
(*She exits out balcony door.*)

CHARLES

Good, generous girl! Carnivals, it seems, don't build character. Well, I guess I'd better go up and see Ricky.

ANNABELLE

Oh, Charles, you're not still worried about Ricky and Connie, are you? Please try not to.

CHARLES

I'll try to worry just the right amount.

ANNABELLE

(*Sighs*)
Sometimes little boys can be so cruel. Or is that too strong a word?

CHARLES

Annabelle, *you* try not to worry too much.

ANNABELLE

(*Putting hand on his shoulder*)
Oh, dear, we are upset, all of us, aren't we?

CHARLES

Yes. We are upset. That was an upsetting thing Ricky did. I wouldn't call that too strong a word.

ANNABELLE

I know. And just when things seemed to be going so
well. I was certain Connie had just about won him over.
That's what distresses me most . . . that I could have been
so very wrong . . .

(*She breaks off as* RICKY *enters on balcony.*)

RICKY

(*Sullen, hostile*)

Janie said you wanted to see me.

CHARLES

(*Rising*)

As a matter of fact, I was just coming up to see you.

RICKY

What for?

CHARLES

I just wanted to say hello. C'mon down. (RICKY *comes
downstairs*) Work on your boat this afternoon?

RICKY

Some.

CHARLES

How's it coming?

RICKY

Okay.

CHARLES

About ready to be launched, I bet.

RICKY

I guess so.

CHARLES

You guess so? You're the Captain.

RICKY

You don't care! What are you asking me for?
(ANNABELLE *and* CHARLES *exchange looks*.)

CHARLES

Ricky, I do care. . . .

RICKY

Miss Annabelle!

ANNABELLE

What is it, dear?

RICKY

Take me to London with you!

ANNABELLE

Darling, you don't mean that!

RICKY

I do! I want to get out of here!

ANNABELLE

Now, Ricky . . .

RICKY

Nobody believes a word I say around here! You all think I'm a liar! But I'm not. Other people lie, though! They lie to me and nothing happens to them! They don't get punished!

CHARLES

Ricky, who lied to you?

RICKY

Connie!

CHARLES

(*Goes to* RICKY)

You must have misunderstood her, Ricky. She wouldn't lie to you. Tell me about it . . . I bet we can straighten it out.

RICKY

No! I hate her! I wish she was dead!

ANNABELLE

Ricky!
(*The doorbell rings.*)

135

CHARLES

(*Grasping* RICKY *by both arms*)

Son, listen to me! (*Sits on chair, still holding* RICKY) We all get mad at each other sometimes. And that temper of yours . . . it's awful big for such a little guy, but I know where you got it . . . (*Jerks a thumb at himself*) But half the time when I get mad at someone . . . it's for nothing . . . I made a mistake . . . I was wrong . . .

RICKY

(*Backing away*)

Connie made the mistake! *She* lied. (*Pulling away from* CHARLES, *crossing to* ANNABELLE) Please, please take me to London with you, please. . . .

CHARLES

Now, Ricky, tell me what happened . . . (*The doorbell rings again*) Damn it . . .

(*He exits into hall.*)

ANNABELLE

Now, dear, you tell Miss Annabelle what really happened.

RICKY

She did lie! She promised to take me to New York with her and then she went without me.

ANNABELLE

Oh, no . . . no, Ricky. You were being punished . . .
(*She sits*) and your punishment was staying at home. Connie
knew that. She never would have promised to take you . . .

RICKY

But she did! Honest! (*Desperately*) Don't *you* believe me,
Miss Annabelle?

ANNABELLE

Of course I do. But I'm terribly afraid that other people
might think that . . .
(*She stops, lets* RICKY *get it.*)

RICKY

You mean Daddy. He won't believe me.

ANNABELLE

Well, now . . .

RICKY

You're right. He'll just think I'm lying again.

ANNABELLE

I'm afraid so. And another little lie might mean more
punishment. So I wouldn't say anything about Connie
promising to take you with her. Ricky . . .

137

RICKY

Yes?

ANNABELLE

(*Conspiratorially*)

Suppose we keep this a secret, you and I.

RICKY

Okay! I'm not going to get punished for nothing again!

ANNABELLE

(*Quickly, hearing* CHARLES *returning*)

We won't tell a soul, will we?

RICKY

No!

(CHARLES *enters, followed by a young man of about thirty.*)

CHARLES

Ricky, would you go to your room for a few minutes, please?

RICKY

Yes, sir.

(*He exits up the stairs.* ANNABELLE *rises.*)

CHARLES

Annabelle, this is Detective Lieutenant Mitchell. Lieutenant, Miss Logan.

138

MITCHELL
(*A greeting*)

Miss Logan.

ANNABELLE

Detective Lieutenant . . . the police? What's gone wrong?

CHARLES

Bad news, I'm afraid. (*Goes to* ANNABELLE, *gently*) It's
Mrs. Walworth. She was hit by a car. She's dead, Annabelle. (ANNABELLE *closes her eyes, stricken.* CHARLES *helps
her into a chair*) I'm sorry. I know what a shock this is.

ANNABELLE

Yes . . . Charles, if I could have some water, please . . .

CHARLES

Yes . . .
(*He exits to hall.*)

MITCHELL

I'm sorry that I . . .

ANNABELLE

No, no . . . (*Urgently*) Tell me . . . when did it happen?

MITCHELL

Just this afternoon.

ANNABELLE

(*Tensely*)

What time this afternoon?

MITCHELL

About one-thirty. (ANNABELLE *stiffens, then covers up by turning away, pretending to be grief-stricken*) I'm sorry, I had to come barging in like this . . .

ANNABELLE

No, I shouldn't have let myself go like this. But it is such a shock. . . .

MITCHELL

Of course.

ANNABELLE

Mrs. Walworth and I . . . we were so very close. . . . The poor soul, where was she?

MITCHELL

King's Highway . . . near the airport. . . . (CHARLES *enters with glass of water*) It seems she'd been drinking. . . .

CHARLES

(*Giving* ANNABELLE *water*)

Here you are.

ANNABELLE

Thank you. (*She sips the water*) I'll be all right now, Charles.

CHARLES

Are you sure?

ANNABELLE

Yes, quite all right. . . .

CHARLES

(*To* MITCHELL)

How did it happen? You said Mrs. Walworth had **been** drinking?

(ANNABELLE *is tense, watchful, dreading the mention of the time of* MRS. WALWORTH'S *death in* CHARLES'S *presence.*)

MITCHELL

Quite a lot. She went into a bar on King's Highway, **the** bartender refused to serve her. She raised quite a fuss, she was pretty drunk, I'm afraid. When she left, she started across the street to another bar. She stepped right in front of a car. The driver didn't have a chance to avoid her . . . The bartender saw it happen.

ANNABELLE

How horrible . . .

CHARLES

I knew she drank some, but I didn't realize it was that bad. Did you notice, Annabelle?

ANNABELLE

(*Quickly*)

No. But then, up to a certain point, she was always in perfect control. The poor thing . . . did she suffer?

MITCHELL

No, she died instantly. Miss Logan, we're hoping you can help us. (*Takes notebook out from inside jacket pocket*) A neighbor of hers told us you've known Mrs. Walworth a long time.

ANNABELLE

(*Nods*)

Almost all my life.

MITCHELL

You're not related to her?

ANNABELLE

No.

MITCHELL

We're trying to locate her family . . . some relative to notify of her death.

ANNABELLE

I'm not sure I can help you. . . .

MITCHELL

(*Referring to notebook*)
Her husband, Harry Walworth. Do you know anything about him?

ANNABELLE

I never knew him. They've been separated for a long time. I have the impression that she lost all track of him years ago.

MITCHELL

What about relatives?

ANNABELLE

None in this country, I'm sure of that. She was English, you know.

MITCHELL

Yes. Her family's there, then.

ANNABELLE

If there is a family . . . It seems she spoke once or twice of a sister . . . no, I can't even be sure of that. It's sad, isn't it, that anyone could be so alone?

MITCHELL

She still heard from somebody in England. . . . (*He takes letter from his pocket*) This letter was in her purse. The return address is . . . (*He reads it*) "17 Melville Street, Knightsbridge, London, S.W. 1 . . ." The writing is obviously a woman's and I think the signature is Lucinda. Does that name mean anything to you, Miss Logan?

(ANNABELLE *rises slowly as* CHARLES *steps to* MITCHELL.)

CHARLES

Lucinda . . . that name's familiar . . . yes, Elizabeth used to speak of a Lucinda . . . Lucinda Marsh, wasn't it?

ANNABELLE

Of course, Lucinda Marsh. Yes!

MITCHELL

She isn't related to Mrs. Walworth?

ANNABELLE

No, no, Mrs. Walworth was Lucinda's nurse way back in England . . . when Lucinda was a child.

MITCHELL

(*To* CHARLES)

You mentioned Elizabeth, Mr. Ashton. That name's here in the letter.

CHARLES

My wife. She died several years ago.

MITCHELL

I see. And then she mentions a Beebee here. . . .

(CHARLES *starts to answer when he is interrupted by* ANNABELLE.)

ANNABELLE

Lieutenant . . . we were such dear friends in the old days, Lucinda and I, we both adored Mrs. Walworth so. It would be much less painful for Lucinda to hear about the accident from me . . . rather than the police.

MITCHELL

I'm sure it would.

ANNABELLE

May I have that letter . . . (*She extends her hand to him*) I'll just copy down the address . . . (*He gives her the letter*) Thank you. Such a sad letter for me to write . . . (*She is crossing to desk*) It will be a shock to Lucinda. Just think . . . she was still writing to Mrs. Walworth after all these years. Such devotion. If only I could have done more.

(*She sits at the desk.*)

CHARLES

(*To* MITCHELL)

Hardly a week passed without Miss Logan visiting Mrs. Walworth. (*Crossing to* ANNABELLE) I'm glad things worked out so that you could be with her this afternoon.

(*He places his hand gently on her shoulder.*)

MITCHELL

This afternoon . . . you saw Mrs. Walworth this afternoon?

ANNABELLE

(*Rising*)

Why, yes, I did.

MITCHELL

What time was that?

ANNABELLE

Well, let me see . . . It was . . . Usually I go for tea, but today things were so confusing here . . . I don't know exactly . . .

CHARLES

You left here when Janie and I did. You must have got to her house a little after three.

MITCHELL

But Mrs. Walworth died about half-past one. I told Miss Logan that. (ANNABELLE *sinks slowly into chair at desk*) In fact, the call came into headquarters at one thirty-five.

CHARLES

(*Goes to* MITCHELL)

That isn't possible. I'm positive Miss Logan didn't leave here until after that. You must be wrong.

MITCHELL

No, sir. It's in the records at headquarters . . . one thirty-five (*To* ANNABELLE) Miss Logan . . .

CHARLES

Just a minute. Who identified Mrs. Walworth?

MITCHELL

Why?

CHARLES

You say she died at one-thirty, but Miss Logan saw her later than that. She spent the afternoon with her. I don't know how it could have happened, but there must have been a mistake in identification. It must have been someone else in the accident.

MITCHELL

(*Taking notebook from breast pocket*)

No, sir.

CHARLES

I know you found Mrs. Walworth's purse, but . . .

MITCHELL

(*Shakes his head*)

There's been no mistake. A neighbor made positive identification. The woman was Ethel Walworth and she died at one-thirty this afternoon.

147

CHARLES

Annabelle . . .

ANNABELLE

(*She rises*)

Charles, Mr. Mitchell, I seem to have made matters worse, not better, as I had hoped. Oh, dear . . . I'm sorry. I'll have to explain. (*She shakes her head*) I didn't go to Mrs. Walworth's at all.

CHARLES

But you said you did.

ANNABELLE

Oh, I meant to go . . . I started out for her house . . . (*To* MITCHELL) When I started thinking about Mrs. Ashton alone here with Ricky. Ricky, that's . . .

MITCHELL

The boy?

ANNABELLE

Yes. (*To* CHARLES) Charles, I was much more upset over what happened this morning than I let you know. To think that Ricky had become capable of so vicious an act . . . I was deeply concerned. So concerned that I didn't go to Ethel Walworth's. I turned around and came back to see if Connie . . . if Connie and Ricky were getting along all right . . .

CHARLES

What did you think could happen?

ANNABELLE

You see, Lieutenant, Ricky blamed Connie for missing the carnival today . . . That was how we punished him for deliberately ruining . . . slashing with a knife Mrs. Ashton's dress. It seemed to make him more resentful than ever . . . as though it were Connie who had punished him, not us. I thought perhaps it was a mistake to leave them alone together all afternoon . . .

CHARLES

It was a mistake.

ANNABELLE

(*Turning to* CHARLES)

No, Charles! Listen to me, let me finish. I was wrong, happily, I was wrong. When I got back here there was Ricky down at the pond playing nice as you please. I was ashamed. I took myself for a long walk and gave myself a good talking to for jumping to such . . . such ridiculous conclusions.

CHARLES

They weren't ridiculous! You heard the way Ricky was carrying on.

ANNABELLE

Charles, he's a little boy! When he says he hates Connie and wishes she were dead . . . he's only a child, making

149

wild, extravagant statements . . . that's all! (CHARLES *turns to her, starts to speak, but she continues*) Oh, can't we discuss this later? Mr. Mitchell's being very patient about our little problem, but I imagine he . . .

MITCHELL

No, it's all right. (*Glances at wrist watch*) Almost five-thirty. I ought to be getting back to headquarters. Sorry I had to bring you bad news . . . but thanks for your help.

CHARLES

Take a short cut to your car across the terrace.

MITCHELL

Thanks, I will. But my hat . . . I left it in the hall.
> (*He makes a move toward the hall.* CHARLES *stops him.*)

CHARLES

I'll get it.
> (*He exits into hall.*)

ANNABELLE

I seem to have upset Mr. Ashton. The very thing I wished to avoid . . . lying about my being at Mrs. Walworth's . . . (*She is at table, touching up flowers*) How very stupid of me!

MITCHELL

(*Awkwardly*)

No . . . I wouldn't say that . . . (*Changes subject, nods toward flowers*) Nice, aren't they? Unusual color.

ANNABELLE

Yes, they are unusual.

MITCHELL

Funny thing. I don't remember ever seeing flowers that color before. And this is the second time today. (*Thinking*) Now where was it . . . ?

ANNABELLE

(*Quickly*)

Lieutenant, tell me . . .

MITCHELL

Oh, yes! At Mrs. Walworth's place, of course. A whole corner of the garden . . .

ANNABELLE

Yes . . . it was she who gave us the bulbs so that we might grow our own.

(CHARLES *enters from hall.*)

CHARLES

Here you are. (*Handing hat to* MITCHELL) I'll walk to your car with you.

(*He starts* MITCHELL *toward terrace.*)

151

MITCHELL

Good-bye, Miss Logan.

ANNABELLE

Good-bye, Lieutenant.

> (MITCHELL *and* CHARLES *exit.* ANNABELLE *has a mo-*
> *ment of near panic. She turns to the vault, then rushes*
> *to it. Viciously, she rips the balloon from the louvered*
> *door. She takes it to the terrace, releases it. As she*
> *watches it rise above the trees, her composure re-*
> *turns. She remembers the letter on the desk. Quickly,*
> *she scans it and she is horrified to see how incrimi-*
> *nating it is. She crumples it up and, as she hears*
> CHARLES *coming back, she thrusts it into her purse on*
> *the desk. When* CHARLES *enters she is at the coffee*
> *table, straightening it up.* CHARLES *goes directly to*
> *the phone, dials Operator.*)

ANNABELLE

Charles, what is it?

CHARLES

(*Into phone*)

Operator . . . New York . . . Atwater 9-1434 . . . (*To*
ANNABELLE) I want to find out what went on here this afternoon.

ANNABELLE

Whom are you phoning?

CHARLES

Connie. She ought to be at Betsy McLane's by now.

ANNABELLE

But is it necessary to worry her before her television show . . . she's nervous enough without you . . . Charles, talk to Ricky, why don't you?

CHARLES

I feel as though I've spent the day cross-examining that kid. (*Into phone*) This is Westford 9-6858. (*Back to* ANNA-BELLE) I want to explain to him why he's wrong . . . that Connie didn't lie to him. (*Into phone*) Hello . . . Betsy, hello. This is Charles Ashton . . . fine, thanks. (ANNA-BELLE *listens, her hands clenched*) Is Connie there? She isn't? She ought to have got to your place by now . . . Yes, she was planning to stop in on her way to the broadcast tonight. Didn't she phone you? Well, she must have changed her mind, then. No . . . no, it's not important . . . (AN-NABELLE *relaxes, smiles*) Yes, I'll tell her. So long.

(*He hangs up.*)

ANNABELLE

I didn't think she'd be there. I believe she was just going to have an early dinner, then go straight on to the studio.

CHARLES

She took the four-eighteen, didn't she?

ANNABELLE

I think that's what she said. Yes, the four-eighteen. Why?

CHARLES

That gets to New York at five-ten.

ANNABELLE

I think so.

CHARLES

That gives her three hours before she has to be at the studio.

ANNABELLE

She wanted to give herself plenty of time.

CHARLES

Three hours? (*He turns to go to desk as* MITCHELL *appears at terrace doors*) Oh, Lieutenant.

MITCHELL

Sorry to bother you again. That letter from England . . . I left it here.

CHARLES

Oh, yes. Annabelle, the letter.

ANNABELLE

Of course. I should have returned it to you . . . (*She
goes to desk*) I left it on the desk when I copied the address . . . (*She looks for the letter.* CHARLES *picks up phone*)
I'm terribly sorry, Lieutenant.

MITCHELL

It's all right. I only got as far as the highway.

CHARLES

Excuse me. . . .
　　(*He is dialing phone.*)

ANNABELLE

Charles! What are you up to now?

CHARLES

Calling the taxi people.

ANNABELLE

Why?

CHARLES

Connie might have taken a later train . . . that's why
she's not at Betsy's . . . (*Into phone*) Hello, this is Charles

Ashton. My wife used one of your cabs to get to the station this afternoon. Could you tell me which train she caught? I'll hold on . . .

ANNABELLE

Charles, why are you so worried?

CHARLES

Let's not keep the Lieutenant waiting, Annabelle.

ANNABELLE

Oh, sorry. I just don't seem to be able to find it. Heavens, the condition I've let this desk get into!
(*She is tidying the desk as she searches for the letter. She puts bills, correspondence into a letter box, her purse into a drawer.* MITCHELL *watches her;* CHARLES *is more involved with the phone call.*)

CHARLES
(*Into phone*)
That's all right. . . . I'll wait . . .

ANNABELLE

Where can it be? Things don't simply vanish into thin air!

MITCHELL
(*Looking at her closely*)
No, they don't.

156

ANNABELLE

Oh, here . . . here's the address! (*Holds it up*) That's all you wanted, isn't it? Lucinda's address. Isn't it lucky I wrote it down! Here you are!

(*She extends it to him.*)

MITCHELL

(*Not taking it*)

Don't you want to make a copy of it? You were so anxious to write to your friend.

ANNABELLE

Oh, yes . . . yes, I do. . . .

(*She jots down the address.*)

CHARLES

(*Into phone.* ANNABELLE *is copying the address, her eyes on* CHARLES)

Yes? You're sure there's no mistake? You see, she was going to . . . Oh, well, then there couldn't possibly be a mistake, could there? Thank you. (*He hangs up*) She didn't take a cab.

MITCHELL

What is it, sir? Something wrong?

CHARLES

I don't know. My wife planned to visit a friend in New York this afternoon . . . she isn't there. That was the taxi company . . .

157

ANNABELLE

Charles, this is being ridiculous . . .

CHARLES

(*Overriding her*)

She didn't take a cab to the station. She didn't even phone for one.

ANNABELLE

She probably got a lift from someone.

CHARLES

(*Picks up phone, dials Operator*)

I suppose that's possible. . . . (*Into phone*) Operator, will you get me the New York Central Station? The ticket office, please.

MITCHELL

Here, let me help you. Tony Coleman's usually on duty this time of day . . . I'll talk to him.

CHARLES

(*Into phone*)

Just a moment.

(*He gives the phone to* MITCHELL.)

ANNABELLE

Lieutenant, you're as bad as he is!

158

MITCHELL

(*Into phone*)

Hello . . . Tony? Al Mitchell. I'm up at the Ashton place. Did Mrs. Ashton . . . you know, Connie Barnes . . . take a train to New York this afternoon? . . . Have you been behind the window all the time? You sure you know Connie Barnes, Tony? Okay. Look, if she was late and had to buy her ticket on the train . . . I see. Okay, thanks. (MITCHELL *hangs up, frowning*) Mrs. Ashton didn't get on any train for New York City this afternoon.

ANNABELLE

Now how can your friend be so positive of that?

MITCHELL

Tony can see the platform from the back window of his office. Not many people got on a New York train this afternoon . . . and Connie Barnes wasn't one of them. Tony is positive.

CHARLES

So, if Connie didn't go to New York . . . where in hell is she?

ANNABELLE

It's foolish of you to be so concerned.

CHARLES

Concerned! My God, I'm a damned sight more than concerned! Why didn't Connie go to New York? And why is

159

Ricky in such a frenzy about her? What in hell happened here this afternoon! (*He starts for stairs*) Is Ricky still in his room?

ANNABELLE

I think so. . . . (CHARLES *exits upstairs.* To MITCHELL) Oh, dear, I suppose I shouldn't blame Mr. Ashton for being upset, but . . .

MITCHELL

Aren't you a little "upset," Miss Logan?

ANNABELLE

(*Carefully*)

Well, I must admit that Mr. Ashton's worry has affected me, yes.

MITCHELL

Is that all? You told me about the boy's resentment of Mrs. Ashton. Didn't you say he slashed a dress of hers?

ANNABELLE

(*Nods*)

That was a very naughty thing for him to do.

MITCHELL

And when you punished him, he resented Mrs. Ashton even more?

ANNABELLE

This *is* a very difficult situation, Lieutenant. Children can be a problem, but for Mr. Ashton to become this alarmed . . . Mrs. Ashton might very well have got a ride all the way into New York or . . .

MITCHELL

Weren't you alarmed? So alarmed that you didn't go to Mrs. Walworth's? You didn't want to leave Ricky and Mrs. Ashton alone together.

ANNABELLE

That's true, but . . .

MITCHELL

What were you afraid of? Weren't you afraid that the boy might hurt Mrs. Ashton?

ANNABELLE

(*Shocked*)
Hurt her? Oh, no . . . I thought there might be some unpleasantness . . . and as it turned out, there was. But I'm sure it was nothing important. You see, I've known little Ricky so well, for so long. . . .

MITCHELL

What was in that letter?

ANNABELLE

(*Stops; turning to* MITCHELL, *startled*)

Letter?

MITCHELL

The one from your friend. . . . Lucinda Marsh. Why did
you take it?

ANNABELLE

But I didn't!

MITCHELL

(*Stepping behind desk, opening drawer*)

It's in your purse, isn't it? You put it there while Mr.
Ashton walked to the car with me. (*Closes drawer sharply*)
What's in that letter? Something about the boy?

ANNABELLE

Why, I've not even read the letter!

MITCHELL

Has Ricky ever been in trouble before? Has he ever hurt
anyone? Is there something about that in the letter?

ANNABELLE

You're imagining all of this . . .

MITCHELL

I don't think so. That's what you're afraid of . . . that
he's hurt Mrs. Ashton. And you're trying to protect him . . .

CHARLES
(*Offstage*)

Ricky!
(RICKY *runs on through the balcony door,* CHARLES *after him.* RICKY *comes downstairs and runs for the terrace.*)

RICKY

No! I won't answer any more questions!

MITCHELL

Ricky!
(RICKY *stops.*)

RICKY

Who are you!

MITCHELL

My name's Al Mitchell, Ricky. Listen, son, we're worried about your mother. . . .

RICKY

My mother!

CHARLES
(*To* MITCHELL)

Connie.

MITCHELL

We're worried about Connie, Ricky. Maybe you can help us.

RICKY

(*Frightened*)

Are you a policeman?

MITCHELL

I'm a detective, yes . . .

RICKY

(*To* CHARLES)

You called the police. . . .

ANNABELLE

Here, let me . . . Look at the state this child's in! (*Her arm around* RICKY) Ricky, dear, we'll go up to my room, just you and I.

(*She starts out with him.*)

MITCHELL

Just a moment please. . . .

CHARLES

(*Comes to* RICKY, *calmly now*)

Rick, I'm sorry I shouted at you, I'm sorry I frightened you. But I don't know where Connie is . . .

RICKY

I don't know anything about her! She went to New York!

164

CHARLES

No . . . she didn't get on the train. She didn't even call a cab. We checked.

RICKY

She did go to New York. She did!

CHARLES

Did you see her leave? Did you say good-bye to her?

RICKY

No, but she went!

CHARLES

She wouldn't leave without saying good-bye to you.

RICKY

She didn't say good-bye on purpose! Because she broke her promise to me!

CHARLES

What did she promise you?

RICKY

(*Turns away, tight-lipped*)

Nothing.

MITCHELL

(*Goes to* RICKY)

Ricky! Where were you when she left?

RICKY

Up in my room.

MITCHELL

Can you see the driveway from there? Did you see a car?

RICKY

No, I didn't see anything. But when I came down she was gone.

CHARLES

You're so sure of that . . . why are you so sure?

RICKY

(*Turning to* CHARLES)

I yelled for her and when she didn't answer, I went looking for her. I looked everywhere and then I knew she was gone when I went and looked . . .

CHARLES

Went and looked where?

RICKY

No place!

CHARLES

What did you see? Where did you look?

166

RICKY

I won't tell you. I'm not going to be punished again.

MITCHELL

Why would he be punished?

ANNABELLE

The poor child . . . please . . .

MITCHELL

(*Insistently*)
Where isn't he allowed to go?

ANNABELLE

Why don't you leave him to me. . . .

CHARLES

(*To* ANNABELLE)
Is there some place he's not allowed to go? (*To* RICKY)
Connie's room . . . is that it? Is it Connie's room you're
not allowed . . . Did you go into Connie's room? I give
you my word you won't be punished. (CHARLES *drops to one
knee before* RICKY) This is more important than that. You
went into Connie's room and you saw something . . . something that made you think Connie had gone. What was it,
Ricky? (RICKY *backs away from* CHARLES) Don't be frightened, Rick . . . I know you didn't do anything wrong . . .
whatever you did was okay, I'm sure it was.

RICKY

(*After a moment*)

All I did was look in her closet! She was going to wear her best clothes to New York and I just looked in her closet to see if her fur coat was gone!

(ANNABELLE *holds her breath.*)

CHARLES

Her fur coat?

RICKY

It's the best of all her clothes. It's the story of her life . . . and it's gone.

CHARLES

And you think she wore it to New York . . . on a day like this?

RICKY

She did!

CHARLES

But it's hot as blazes today. . . .

RICKY

She took her fur coat! Look for yourself!

CHARLES

(*Slowly*)

No. She was going to put it away . . . (*Pause*) She was going to store it. . . .

(*He turns slowly toward the vault.*)

168

ANNABELLE

(*Quickly*)

No, Charles, she changed her mind . . . she took it into New York to have it altered . . .

CHARLES

(*Going to vault*)

She might have put it in the vault . . .

(*He opens the outer doors, tries the steel door.*)

ANNABELLE

No, I spoke to her yesterday about storing it, but there was some work she wanted done first. . . .

CHARLES

(*Going to desk*)

The combination, it's in the desk. . . .

(MITCHELL *moves up to the vault, examines the door.* RICKY *turns to watch* CHARLES *at the desk.*)

ANNABELLE

Yes, it's in the top drawer. Now you'll see how absurd you're being. . . .

CHARLES

(*Searching for it*)

Annabelle, where is it . . . ?

ANNABELLE

Right there . . . it's always been there.

CHARLES

You know the combination . . .

ANNABELLE

No. No, I've never known it.

MITCHELL

Doesn't anyone remember the combination?
(*A pause.*)

ANNABELLE

Ricky, dear, go upstairs.

CHARLES

Yes, Ricky, go upstairs. (RICKY *runs halfway upstairs, then hides, crouching down against the wall*) It isn't here ... I can't find it . . .

MITCHELL

Somebody must know the combination!

CHARLES

No! It's always been here in the desk . . .
(MITCHELL *picks up the phone and dials* "0.")

ANNABELLE

Lieutenant, listen to me! She couldn't be in there! She couldn't have opened the vault!

MITCHELL

(*Into phone*)

Get me the police . . . quickly . . .

ANNABELLE

She doesn't know the combination!

CHARLES

(*Slowly, reasoning it out*)

The combination was on a paper in the desk. It's gone now. She could have found it and used it . . . taken it into the vault with her . . .

MITCHELL

(*Into phone*)

This is Mitchell . . . Emergency!

ANNABELLE

(*To* MITCHELL)

Of course, you're right. We must make sure.

MITCHELL

(*Into phone*)

Emergency . . . at the Ashton place . . . Charles Ashton, up on the hill . . . We're afraid someone is locked in a vault

. . . that's right . . . Get the Emergency Squad here immediately . . . Right.

> (*He hangs up.*)

CHARLES

How soon can they get here?

MITCHELL

Ten minutes . . . maybe sooner.

CHARLES

Thank God!

ANNABELLE

Lieutenant, how long will it take to get it open?

MITCHELL

I don't know. It won't be easy. How thick are those walls?

CHARLES

Fourteen inches . . . sixteen maybe . . .

MITCHELL

It could take hours. . . . (ANNABELLE *turns away in relief.* CHARLES *slowly turns toward vault, then quickly goes to it listening at door*) How big is that vault?

CHARLES

> (*Turning to* MITCHELL)

About four by four . . . seven feet high . . .

MITCHELL

How long could she have been in there?

CHARLES

I don't know . . . We left here at three . . .

MITCHELL

(*Looks at wrist watch*)
Five-thirty . . . (*Almost to himself*) They'll have to work fast!

CHARLES

I don't understand how it happened. How could anyone get caught in there? That door can only be locked from the outside. (*Goes to* ANNABELLE) Annabelle, maybe you're right . . . she isn't in there . . . She couldn't have locked herself in there!

ANNABELLE

Of course not! Charles, stop torturing yourself. . . .

MITCHELL

Exactly—someone would have had to lock her in!

CHARLES

What did you say?

MITCHELL

She would have to be . .
(*He stops, seeing* CHARLES's *reaction.*)

CHARLES

(*Moves slowly to desk, picks up letter*)
Connie's dog . . . it suffocated . . .

ANNABELLE

Charles, what are you thinking . . . ?

MITCHELL

(*Takes letter from* CHARLES. *Looks at it*)
Her dog was suffocated? (*To* ANNABELLE) That's what
you were hiding. . . . The boy put the dog in the vault . . .
(*Suddenly*) Then he knows the combination!

ANNABELLE

No! No, he doesn't . . .

MITCHELL

Get him down here . . .

ANNABELLE

He didn't do it! He didn't kill the dog!

MITCHELL

Get the boy down here.

ANNABELLE

Ricky doesn't know how to open the vault!

MITCHELL

Then, how was it opened?

ANNABELLE

He had nothing to do with it! I opened it! I left it open
. . . it was stupid of me! It was my fault the dog died . . .
entirely my fault!

MITCHELL

Look, Miss Logan . . .

RICKY

(*Running down the stairs*)
Miss Annabelle! It wasn't your fault!
(*All turn to him.*)

ANNABELLE

Ricky!

RICKY

Don't you take the blame, Miss Annabelle! (*He hugs*
ANNABELLE *protectingly*) You leave her alone. She didn't
do it, I did it!

CHARLES

Ricky, Connie is in the vault . . .

RICKY

I didn't do anything to Connie! I didn't shut her in! I
didn't do anything to her!

CHARLES

Unless we get her out of there, she'll die. You don't want
that to happen, do you?

RICKY

I didn't do it! I didn't do it!

CHARLES

You know the combination! Open the door, Ricky!

RICKY

(*Sobbing wildly, he flings himself at* CHARLES
beating his fists against CHARLES's *chest*)
You'll blame me for it. You blame me for everything.
You'll blame me!

CHARLES

(*Holding* RICKY *in his arms*)
Oh, God! (*Distant siren is heard.* CHARLES *speaks softly
to* RICKY) It's all right, son, it's all right. You didn't mean
it, whatever happened, you didn't mean it. Of course you
didn't . . . (*He walks with his arm around* RICKY *toward
the vault. The siren is heard closer*) Now we'll get Connie
out of there and everything will be all right. Ricky, you
know the combination. Let's open the vault. (*They are in
front of the vault*) What's the first number, Ricky?

(ANNABELLE *turns slowly toward the vault, stands
frozen, waiting.*)

RICKY

Twenty-eight . . .

CHARLES

Do it, Ricky . . .

RICKY

First you turn it to twenty-eight . . .

CHARLES

And then? Do you turn it back?

RICKY

Yes . . . back to eleven . . . like that . . . Wait, first twenty-eight . . . back to eleven . . . and thirty-two . . . That's it, there!

(RICKY *steps back and* CHARLES *wrenches open the vault door.* CONNIE *stumbles out;* CHARLES *catches her. Siren is heard coming nearer.* MITCHELL *helps* CHARLES *lift* CONNIE *into his arms.* CHARLES *carries her to the sofa.* CONNIE *leans against the back of the sofa, her eyes closed, gasping for air.* RICKY *runs to* ANNABELLE.)

RICKY

Is she all right, will she be all right . . . ?

MITCHELL

(*At* CONNIE's *side*)

Yes, she'll be all right. (*The siren stops outside.* MITCHELL *exits.*)

CONNIE

(*Whispering*)

Ricky . . .

CHARLES

(*Turns away from* CONNIE *to* RICKY,
beckons him to them)

Ricky . . .

ANNABELLE

(*Goes to table behind sofa*)

Some brandy . . .

RICKY

(*Kneels before* CONNIE)

Connie, tell them I didn't do it, please, tell them . . .

CONNIE

(*Taking* RICKY *in her arms*)

No, Ricky, you didn't do it. It wasn't you. It wasn't you...
(*Another siren in the distance is heard.* ANNABELLE
*slips quickly into the vault, pulls the door almost
closed after her.*)

CHARLES

(*Rising slowly from sofa*)

Annabelle . . .

(MITCHELL *enters, followed by a* POLICEMAN *in uniform.*)

CHARLES

Annabelle! She's gone! (MITCHELL *runs out the hall door; the* POLICEMAN *runs out the terrace doors.* CHARLES *starts for the stairs, then stops. He looks at* CONNIE, *then at the vault. He goes to the vault*) Keep this damn door locked! (*He slams shut the steel door, locks it and closes the louvered doors*) I'll have it sealed up tomorrow . . .

(*He starts toward* CONNIE *and* RICKY.)

Curtain